How to Try a Jury Trial

How to Try a Jury Trial

David Crump

qp

QUID PRO BOOKS

New Orleans, Louisiana

Published in 2025 by Quid Pro Books.

ISBN 978-1-61027-530-9 (trade paperback)
ISBN 978-1-61027-525-5 (mass mkt. pbk.)

QUID PRO BOOKS
Quid Pro, LLC
5860 Citrus Blvd., ste. D
New Orleans, Louisiana 70123
www.quidprobooks.com

This information is provided to aid comprehension of practice and procedure, and should not be construed as legal advice or the practice of law. Please consult an attorney for inquiries regarding legal matters.

Publisher's Cataloging-in-Publication

Crump, David.

    How to Try a Jury Trial / David Crump.

      p. cm.

    Includes appendix, forms, and examples.

I. Trial Practice—United States. 2. Jury—United States. I. Title.

KF8195 .C43 2025

Table of Contents

PREFACE

This Book Isn't about Intricacies in the Rules of Evidence or Procedure.[1] It's about how to do it. How to try a jury trial. Hands on. Strategically. The Rules are baked into it, of course, because the Rules are a part of a successful trial, but that's not the primary focus.

Instead, the School of Hard Knocks is where this advice comes from. From the author's trials of many cases, winning some and losing some. You learn from both types.

I expect that experienced trial lawyers will agree with most of the advice here, but every lawyer will probably find some points of disagreement too. That can't be avoided in this kind of book. I've written what I know, and obviously, I don't know enough to avoid differences among lawyers.

The book comes from my jurisdiction. In fact, it comes from the most heavily populated city in this state. Our people are diverse. Many of them come from other states. But I suspect that juries everywhere have a lot in common. They have regional differences too, but the same evidence and arguments can be used to persuade them.

And So, My Mission in These Pages is to help you get ready to try jury trials. And to try them successfully.

---

[1] I have books that do that: teaching books for law school. *E.g.*, David Crump et al., *Civil Procedure: Cases, Materials, and Lawyering Strategies* (2019); Paul Rothstein, David Crump, & Tamara Lawson, *Evidence: Cases, Materials, and Problems* (2019). But those books don't tell you how to do it.

How to Try
a Jury Trial

Chapter 1

YOUR TRIAL NOTEBOOK AND OTHER MATTERS ON THE EVE OF TRIAL

CONTENTS OF THE TRIAL NOTEBOOK

Historically, lawyers made trial notebooks in three-ring binders filled with physical sheets of paper. Nowadays it is likely to be an electronic notebook inside a laptop. But the organization is the same as the old-fashioned version, and it is useful to illustrate the methods of a trial notebook by assuming it will be on paper.

What will the contents be like, then?

In Part 1, the First Page Is Witness Contacts. Part One is about matters on the eve of the trial. This Part starts with a page that is filled with information about how to contact your witnesses.

Don't minimize this seemingly simple step. Many trial lawyers find that getting the bodies of their witnesses into the courtroom is a nightmare, precipitating real stomach acid. And so, for every witness, there should be multiple ways of contact. If you have both an office landline and a mobile phone number, include both here, and a home telephone too. If the guy or lady has a secretary who arranges all the meetings, write out the secretary's name and number too.

Include the witnesses' addresses. I once knew about a case in which one of the junior lawyers had to drive out to the witness's home. The witness could not be reached by telephone; the phone went consistently to voicemail. The messenger lawyer found the witness happily cutting his huge lawn on a riding mower and hustled him to the courtroom, still wearing his grass-working togs.

So, the names of the witnesses go down the page vertically, and next to each name are the multiple contact methods. Witnesses needing to be subpoenaed have already been subpoenaed, of course, but you'd better call them too. Junior lawyers and paralegals are part of the team, but getting the witnesses bodily to the courtroom is so important and unreliable that the lead lawyer has got to be involved. He or she may have to get on the phone with a lead witness and say, forcefully, but sounding friendly of course, "We've been called to trial. This is it! Get here, please, as quickly as Batman!"

A representation of this witness page appears in the mock trial notebook, which appears in an appendix at the end of this book.

The First Part also Includes Motions on the Eve of Trial. Motions in Limine are an example. In nearly every case at least one party should file a Motion in Limine asking for exclusion of at least one type of inadmissible evidence unless a hearing produces an order of the court to the contrary. Settlement offers and liability insurance are frequent types. The defendant, particularly, may want to file such a motion about either or both of these issues.

Just put the motion itself into the notebook. If the motion is lengthy, more than, say, three pages, just put the front page and a second page. But you shouldn't file anything that long anyway on the eve of trial. On the other hand, include in your Motion in Limine any kind of inadmissible evidence that is special to your case and that might come up.

What other motions will go into this slot? Maybe a motion for continuance in case there is a problem discovered at the last moment. Repetition of a motion for severance, if needed. A Motion in Limine favoring the admissibility of a specific piece of evidence that you want to offer but that you know is contested by the other side. A *Daubert* Motion, if the admissibility of an expert opinion arises late in the case.

Second, Voir Dire Notes, in Part 2. A second part of the trial notebook includes your notes for voir dire. See the appendix at the end of this book. I assume that you are going to be doing a state-type voir dire (attorneys doing most of the questioning) because that is what I've encountered, in both federal and state courts. See chapter 2.

Third, Opening Statement, in Part 3. The next section, section 3, contains your notes for your opening statement, set out in an outline. I myself tended to write out the opening statement completely and keep it in this place. But for you, I say, don't do that. I was able to take the notes with me when I stood in front of the jury, and I could give the opening statement while glancing at it but without reading it. Normally, the lawyer should have it in outline form because if you write it out you'll tend to read it, and that's deadly. See the example in the appendix.

Fourth, Witness Examination Outlines, in Part 4. Here, you'll have a single page for each witness. In outline form. Including witnesses you intend to cross-examine. See the appendix and Chapter 4.

Fifth, Directed Verdict, in Part 5. Here, you'll have a motion for directed verdict, or for judgment as a matter of law, for whichever court you are in, if there is any possibility of its being applicable. See the appendix and Chapter 5.

Sixth, Court's Charge in Part 6. Insert your requests for jury instructions and charges. (You prepared these early in the case if you followed widespread advice, before you started discovery. Revise them as needed.) See the appendix and Chapter 6.

And Finally, Seventh, Final Arguments, Part 7. You should include your preliminary notes for your final argument, in an outline form. See the appendix and Chapter 7.

IN THE APPENDIX AT THE END OF THIS BOOK,
I'VE INCLUDED AN OUTLINE OF A TRIAL NOTEBOOK.

A CASE TO SERVE AS AN EXAMPLE

Here Is a Case that We Will Use Throughout the Book. Plaintiffs Daniel and Meredith Smith are suing John Anton. The plaintiffs' witnesses say that Anton drove his motorcycle in a school zone at 3:15 p.m. at speeds estimated at 50 to 65 mph by a police officer, Officer Hauseshorn, and by Meredith Smith. He collided with little Sarah Smith, their six-year-old daughter, and killed her while she was walking home from school. They have an economist and themselves to testify to damages, which they claim exceed $10 million.

Anton's defense includes a witness who followed Anton, who will testify that Anton was going slowly, under the 20-mph speed limit. The child darted into the street, he claims, and he couldn't stop. The defense also says that the damages claim is way exaggerated.

Chapter 2

VOIR DIRE AND JURY SELECTION

INVOKING THE RULE: SEQUESTRATION OF WITNESSES

First, remember to invoke the Rule, if it's to your advantage. In the federal system, it's in Federal Rule of Evidence 615. It means that the judge instructs the witnesses to remain outside the courtroom and, usually, to avoid discussing the case except with the attorneys. It's designed to prevent witnesses from conforming their testimony to each other's testimony.

And when is it to your advantage to invoke the Rule? There can be many factors, but usually the big one is when your opponent has more witnesses who have to remain outside than you have. The parties, plaintiff and defendant, are permitted in the courtroom, of course, including a representative of a business entity (a corporation, partnership, etc.). Sometimes the court will permit an expert witness or a case officer to remain (like an FBI agent who assists one of the attorneys).

So, for example, think about the case we've discussed in Chapter 1: *Smith v. Anton.* There are two plaintiffs and one defendant who will be permitted to remain in the courtroom. Plaintiff has four additional witnesses. Defendant has only one additional witness. The defendant would probably invoke the Rule because the plaintiff has more witnesses whom the defendant can prevent from listening to each other.

To invoke the Rule, stand up and say, "Your honor, we invoke the Rule."

ASK THE JUDGE HOW HE/SHE DOES JURY SELECTION

There are infinitely many ways to conduct jury selection, and the method affects the way you do voir dire. If the court has you examine one venireperson at a time with challenges one by one, that's different from addressing a panel. Ask the judge in the case, as early as possible, how he or she does it. Or consult with experienced local counsel.

REMEMBER OUR CASE USED FOR ILLUSTRATION

Here is the case that we are using throughout the book.

Plaintiffs Daniel and Meredith Smith are suing John Anton. The plaintiffs' witnesses say that Anton drove his motorcycle in a school zone at 3:15 p.m. at speeds estimated at 50 to 65 mph by a police officer, Officer Hauseshorn, and by Meredith Smith. He collided with little Sarah Smith, their six-year-old daughter, and killed her while she was walking home from school. They have an economist and themselves to testify to damages, which they claim exceed $ 10 million.

Anton's defense includes a witness who followed Anton himself, who will testify that he was going slowly, under the 20-mph speed limit. The child darted into the street, Anton claims, and he couldn't stop. The defense also says that the damages claim is far exaggerated.

VOIR DIRE IN THIS CASE

The voir dire itself commences with your standing before the jury (or at a podium, if the court uses one) and saying,

> "Good morning, ladies and gentlemen of the jury. I'm David Garrison, and I represent the plaintiffs. That's Meredith Smith, here, and Daniel Smith. Stand up, Daniel. Stand up, please, Meredith. They are the most important people in the room, for me. Does anyone see anything about them that you don't like, that would make us start the race ten yards back, so to speak?

> "Now, this is a case in which I expect the evidence to show that John Anton, over there (pointing emphatically at Anton), drove his motorcycle at 50 to 65 miles per hour in a school zone at 3:15 and killed their daughter, little Sarah, six years old. He was grossly negligent, as the law would say it. Mr. Firstjuror, could you be a juror and return a verdict in a case like this?"

You do these introductions even if the judge has introduced everyone; you do it again. With these words, you've (1) personalized your clients a little (more will come later), and (2) you've introduced your case. In a partisan way, of course. It's an adversary system, and the battle starts right at the beginning.

Incidentally, does the lawyer suggest that he or she is biased or leaning toward misleading the jurors by saying they're his friends or that they are the most important in the courtroom? Maybe. But more likely, the lawyer suggests that these plaintiffs are worthy of the lawyer's efforts and, therefore, they probably have a good case. (Reasoning by jurors in the courtroom is sometimes like this.)

If you represent the defense, you do the same things, sort of "in reverse," so to speak. You introduce your client similarly, and you introduce your case similarly but the opposite way. "I don't see the case the same way as my friend David Garrison. He left out a few things. This is a case where John Anton was proceeding slowly and carefully, below the 20-mph speed limit, and the child darted out right in front of him, and he tried to stop, but he couldn't. John was not negligent, not anywhere close to it."

If you represent the defense, you are going to end up trying the victims. And attacking the victims.

STRATEGIES AND TACTICS IN VOIR DIRE

There are strategies and tactics that lawyers use to gain advantage during the voir dire examination of the potential jurors. I've always practiced in courts that have permitted voir dire by the attorneys, sometimes referred to as "state-court voir dire." Both in federal and state courts. And this set of tactics assumes that.[2]

Your strategy, of course, is to weed out venirepersons who'd be bad for your case. And there are tactics for that. But you also want to persuade, to the extent that the law allows. You want to paint a horrifying picture of the other side's conduct and of what happened, favoring your side. You want the law to be applied so as to favor you. And you want to be diplomatic with the jurors—they're going to decide for you or against you!—and deferential to them.

---

[2] *See* Simmons v. Napier, 626 Fed. Appx. 129 (6th Cir. 2015) (unpublished opinion) (discussing the difference between state-type voir dire, which usually is conducted by the lawyers, and federal practice, which allows the judge either to perform the entire voir dire or to let the attorneys do all or part of it).

You are a supplicant, when you speak to the jury.

Let me repeat that, because it's important. You are a supplicant, when you speak to a jury. You are very, very polite, diplomatic, and humble. You are a supplicant.

So: What are these strategies and tactics?[3]

They range from introducing the client and preparing jurors to accept the proof, to increasing or lowering the standards in the law. And they always include diplomacy and praising the jurors.

Here, I will first set out some basic strategies. And then, in a later section I will provide some examples that illuminate the ethics and the execution of the strategies.

First, basic strategies and tactics:

Thanking the Jurors. A lawyer might begin by thanking the potential jurors, like this.

> "Ladies and gentlemen, I'd like to thank you for being here, when many of us would like to be somewhere else. You are performing that great civic duty that we learned in civics class long ago. You are part of the American miracle. Juries don't exist in totalitarian countries, and I know that everyone here appreciates you."

Some people feel that this beginning is just a distraction, but I'm convinced they're wrong. Experiments in psychology have shown that "audience reward," as it's called, is a major influence in attraction theory.[4] We like people who like us back.[5]

Also, there are lawyers who think that jurors will take this passage as phony. But once more, psychologists have done amazing experiments that show that they won't think it's phony.[6] Experimental subjects attribute words of even an actor

---

[3] *Cf.* David Crump, *Attorneys' Goals and Tactics in Voir Dire Examination,* 43 Tex. B.J. 244 (1980), *referenced at* https://caplaw.com/sites/cp7; and click on Document Example 10.1 (last visited June 1, 2025), for a different view of these issues.

[4] *See* David Crump, How to Reason 353 (2014) (describing experimental findings that the audience-reward theory increases the listener's reception of the message).

[5] *Cf. id.* (describing use of the technique by a hypothetical car salesperson).

[6] *See id.* at 352-53 (describing the Napolitan-Goethals experiment). The remarkable result was that people who were told openly that a particular speaker would be acting as either "friendly" or "cold"—merely acting—nevertheless attributed her attitude to her real personality, not to her acting, which they were informed about. This well-informed group showed no statistical difference from a control group who were not informed at all about the speaker's acting.

with a known agenda to the actor's sincere attitude, rather than to the actor's agenda. This psychological result means that the jurors will take the lawyer's words as sincere, even though they know the lawyer has a purpose for saying them.

Presenting the Client. A lawyer will want to humanize his client, but the lawyer will want to do more than that.[7]

> "This is my *friend*, Clark Client, here." [To the client:] "Stand up, Clark, please." "Now, Clark is similar to you; he lives right here in Springfield. He's lived his whole life here. Now, does anyone see anything about Clark, my friend, that would make you question him at all about his belief in his case? I don't see any hands and I didn't expect to. But you know, Clark is the most important person here, to me, and so that's why I ask."

It's analogous if the lawyer represents a corporation or other business entity. Then, the lawyer has an attractive spokesperson from the company sit at the table.

> "This is Diane Wilson, and she's from the plaintiff/defendant, Jamison Company. That doesn't mean she owns the whole company—Sorry, Diane—but she handles issues like this, in public business."[8] Anyone see anything about Diane that looks like you'd be against her?

During the trial, the lawyer calls Jamison Company "Diane's company."

Conditioning the Jurors to Favor Your Evidence. You may be able to prepare the jurors to accept your side of the story. "Ms. Jones, may I be permitted to ask you a couple of questions? (The answer you hope for is "Yes" or "Sure." If Ms. Jones seems too scared to do it right, go to the next juror.)

> "Ms. Jones, the law says that a single witness is enough to prove a case, if you believe him or her. Now, Ms. Jones, could you follow the law and decide the case in favor of someone offering you a single witness, if you believed that witness?" (Yes, I think so.)

Then, "Thank you Ms. Jones. Now, to everyone else on this jury panel, could you do the same as Ms. Jones? Anyone who couldn't?"

Some courts will disallow this kind of questioning, especially if you ask

---

The experiment demonstrated the "fundamental attribution error," which makes people attribute behavior to an actor's "disposition," or real personality, rather than "situationally," or taking into account the circumstances.

[7] *See id.* at 353 (describing attraction theory, which includes experimental results showing that familiarity and identification enhance attraction). We tend to like those whom we know and who are similar to us.

[8] *See id.* at 354 (presenting a familiar and attractive spokesperson enhances persuasion).

jurors to "commit" to finding in favor of your case. But if you ask in terms of what the law requires and put it in the abstract rather than in terms of the facts of your case, you have a much better chance of having the court permit it.[9]

And the ringer is that the lawyer actually has not one witness but several, and now has a promise to at least consider believing them. And you might add, "But I expect that in reality, we will prove our case with more than just one witness, but even if you believe only one of them . . . ."[10]

And imagine that the lawyer has a whole lot of evidence but expects the opponent to object to large parts of it. Then, the lawyer says, "I'm going to bring all the evidence to you. All of it. I think that's the best way to decide a case. And I hope Mr. Opponent will be doing the same thing, getting all the facts to you." In fact, however, the lawyer expects his opponent to do the exact opposite by objecting to everything. And he hopes the jury will see Mr. Opponent as trying to "hide" something (which he is).

What if your evidence is thin? With witnesses who are scared and uncertain? Then your approach is different:

> "Ladies and gentlemen, I don't like how some lawyers drag things out. Lawyers sometimes put on a complete dog-and-pony show when it's not called for. And so, we've taken our case and boiled it down to the essentials. We'll bring you all the evidence that's relevant—but we've boiled it down to avoid the dog-and-pony show."

And this lawyer is hoping the opponent won't respond with, "Boiled it down? Boiled it down? They just have a weak case, and they've now admitted it. They didn't boil it down; they just have no case."

And then, there is the issue of damages:

> "I expect the evidence to show that the damages to Diane's company exceed 250 million dollars. All caused by Opponent Corporation. I know it sounds like a huge amount—certainly a lot more than my bank account! And I'm guessing that it's more than your bank account, Ms. Green; am I right? Now, Ms. Green, I need to ask: Do you have an opinion before we start, that 250

---

[9]*See* Robert R. Barton, Fundamentals of Texas Trial Law 42 (3d ed. 2009) (stating that it is improper to ask potential jurors to "commit" to a position based on a set of circumstances analogous to this case). *Cf.* Cortez *ex rel.* Estate of Puente v. HCCI San Antonio, Inc., 159 S.W.3d 87 (Tex. 2005) (giving judge significant power over voir dire).
[10] This is "framing" or setting the agenda. *See* David Crump, *supra* note 4, at 354.

million dollars is too much? That you couldn't award 250 million in damages, if it were proved to you?"

The defendant might respond by saying,

"Everything about the plaintiff's case is exaggerated, and it's all inflated, including that bit about '250 million dollars' or whatever. If they got 250 million dollars, they could divide it up with everybody in the company to invest in municipal bonds, and they'd all live a fabulously rich life forever."

Obtaining Commitments: Some Courts Disallow It. Some courts permit a lawyer to obtain commitments from the jurors based on the evidence: a promise of a particular outcome:

"When they did this merger, the defendant company got the merging company to give indemnities to all its personnel. An indemnity is a promise to pay all of the personnel's damages. You see, they knew they were doing something wrong. Mr. Johnson, can you consider these indemnities as evidence that they knew they were doing something wrong?"

Other courts—maybe the majority—disallow this kind of thing, obtaining commitments to view the evidence in certain ways. But even there, some lawyers can skillfully, even if dishonorably, sneak it in, especially if the opposing lawyer is asleep at the switch and doesn't object.[11]

Discussing the Law So as to Increase the Standard—Or Decrease It. A personal injury plaintiff's lawyer may set out the essential point in the law to make it easier to win.

"The judge will define 'negligence' by saying something like this: 'Negligence means doing that which a reasonable person would do or not doing that which a reasonable person would do, in the exercise of ordinary care.'[12]

"Now, that's a whole bunch of legal terms. In ordinary language, negligence

---

[11] Believe it or not, this colloquy, paraphrased here, was used by well-known lawyer Joe Jamail in the trial of Texaco Co. v. Pennzoil Inc., 784 F.2d 1133 (2d Cir. 1986), which produced the then-largest damage verdict in history. *See* Voir Dire by Joseph D. Jamail in Pennzoil Inc. v. Texaco Co., No. 84-05905, 151st Dist. Ct., Harris Cty., Tex., July 10, 1985, *excerpted at* Litigation Document Example 10.1, *supra* note 3, at 5.

[12] *Cf.* State Bar, Texas Pattern Jury Charges, PJC 2.1-2.2, at https://texashistory.unt.edu/ark:/67531/metapth639249/hits/?q=negligence+definition+PJC+2.2 (last visited June 1, 2025) (containing a more complete definition, which the hypothetical lawyer paraphrases in the text above).

means *carelessness*. Just plain *carelessness* is the issue in this case."[13]

The defense lawyer will translate them differently. "Negligence means someone is *guilty of an un-reas-onable act*. See, the word 'carelessness' isn't in there at all.*"*

Why? Well, I often use the analogy of a pole vaulter, trying to get over a high bar. If it's too high, you can do either of two things. You can get a longer pole—by analogy, that means getting more evidence. Or you can lower the bar—and that's what the plaintiff's lawyer is trying to do here, by saying that "negligence is just carelessness."

"Negligence" sounds harsh. It makes it almost seem like a crime, like negligent homicide. Hard for a jury to find; harder for a juror to pin on a defendant. "Carelessness" sounds so much easier to use as a label on a defendant. And on the opposite side, the defense lawyer is trying to make the bar even higher than it otherwise sounds, by using words like "guilty" of an "unreasonable act." The defense lawyer's trying to make it sound even more like a crime.

This tactic can be used in any kind of case. Just study the court's instructions and verdict forms and think about a translation into simpler language. Imagine a contract case. The plaintiff might read the judge's legalistic language to the jury defining a contract and then say, "All it means is, like a handshake in the oil patch. That's what makes a contract, that handshake that seals the deal."[14] In the footnote, I've included some other informal, folksy translations of contract terminology into easier-to-prove English words.

Building Rapport. "I practice law on my own, what we call a solo practitioner, and over there on the other side, at Dewey Cheatum and Howe, they have more than 400 attorneys, all well paid, so I'd like to ask, Does anyone here know someone who works for Dewey Cheatum and Howe?" On occasion, the tactic gets expanded: "Mr. Opposing Lawyer, just how many lawyers does Dewey Cheatum and Howe have all over the world?" But be careful; with this kind of thing, you risk having your speech get too big. And you risk having your opponent respond with something that takes all the effectiveness out of your voir dire.

---

[13] This formula is used to explain negligence in popular sources. "Negligence involves harm caused by . . . a form of *carelessness* . . . . " Wikipedia, https://en.wikipedia.org/wiki/Negligence (last visited June 1, 2025).

[14] Contract cases: "breach" just means "they made a promise and then broke it." As for contract formation: "Even a handshake is enough to create a contract, but we will show you a signed document, signed by this defendant." Securities cases: "They omitted information 'required to make their statements not misleading.' That just means they didn't tell you something bad, and that bad thing made you lose your shirt."

The opponent responds by saying, "Ms. Plaintiff's Lawyer (or Defendant's) acts like she's the underdog. On the contrary, let me tell you, she is a very experienced and capable trial lawyer who can influence juries. Don't let her influence you, because that so-called 'underdog' knows how to bite!"

I have a friend who once represented Shell Oil Company as a defendant. He asked the jury, "Now, would anyone be prejudiced against Shell because it employs 20,000 people in this area?" "Would anyone be prejudiced against Shell because it generates billions in income for the people in our city?" "Will anyone be prejudiced against Shell because it sponsors the Shell Open Golf Tournament here?" And so on. Helpful propaganda is wherever you find it.

Humor. Even corny, marginal humor works in the stern atmosphere of the courtroom. Jurors are leery of lawyers anyway. So, the defendant says,

"Please, I beg you, wait until we, the defendant, present our case.

"As the old mountain man said about his pancakes, 'No matter how thin I make 'em, there are always two sides.'"

"And I know you've been herded around and told to sit a long time on these benches here. I think they order special, extra-hard benches for these courtrooms."

This kind of corny comedy sometimes will draw broad smiles from the potential jurors. That is, if you do it right. Be bold. And informal. Jurors like looser, more relaxed lawyers more than uptight ones.

Arguing (or Framing) the Case. Unver the law, voir dire is for jury selection, not for arguing the case. But the lawyer has to give the jurors the basic facts for them to be able to answer questions, and inevitably, the case is presented strategically. The result is that voir dire becomes like an opening statement.[15] But a very *brief* opening statement. The plaintiff's lawyer might say,

"Ladies and gentlemen, we will show you three themes.

First, the defendant drove his motorcycle not just fast, but way too fast— like, fifty to sixty miles per hour—in a school zone.

Second, the defendants are going to try to blame the child that he killed, but

---

[15] This is another form of framing. The lawyer who persuades the jury about framing has not yet won the case but has selected the battleground: the issues that will be important in the trial.

that's wrong, because the child didn't do anything other than what a normal child would do.

Third, it would take more than ten million dollars to compensate for this awful loss to Mr. and Mrs. Smith."[16]

Thus, the plaintiff has introduced the negligence of the driver, freedom from contributory negligence of the plaintiffs' decedent, and the amount of damage.

The defendant will answer with a different three themes: "The driver was proceeding carefully, the child darted out, and even the damage amount is inflated."

Inoculation. Whenever there's a bad fact, and it's bound to come into evidence against you, you're better off talking about it upfront and treating it so that it's not as bad.[17] This tactic is called "inoculation." In medicine, inoculation means giving the patient a little dose of the same disease you're trying to prevent, in a weakened form. And it's the same tactic in voir dire.

The usual illustration is to imagine that your client has a felony conviction that is going to come into evidence to impeach your client at trial. The judge has overruled your motion in limine and said it's admissible. So, during voir dire, you say,

"Now, I want to tell you something else that you will hear from Mr. Opponent. I think it is unfortunate that he will do this. Many years ago, Clark Client made a mistake, and he got convicted in misdemeanor criminal court for it. Or rather, he stood up in court and admitted it. And he was sentenced to probation, which means you're walking on eggshells, but he served out his probation and made a good life.

"I think his honor the judge will tell you that you can consider this for credibility, but you cannot use it to decide that Clark is or was a bad man and you can't hold against him because of it. Is there anyone who can't

---

[16] Naming a specific amount is important. It introduces the phenomenon of "anchoring": listeners may not accept the exact figure, but the statement provides an "anchor" that guides the jury.

[17] Some scholars have reported that "attorneys use voir dire to . . . inoculate the jury against opposing evidence that may be presented later in the case. " Jill M. Leibold, Ph.D, *Making the Case for Attorney-Conducted Voir Dire to Promote Juror Candor in Open Court,* https://www.litigationinsights.com/making-the-case-for-the-benefits-of-attorney-conducted-voir-dire-to-promote-juror-candor-in-open-court (last visited January 6, 2021).

follow that instruction?"[18]

This is inoculation. You've given the jury a little amount of the evidence that is bad news for you. And you've weakened its harshness. You've done it all forthrightly, so that you appear credible to the jury.

Suggesting How the Jury Should Deliberate (a Rare Tactic). Sometimes a lawyer will nominate the foreperson or presiding juror.

> "Mr. Johnson, it might be that you could be elected to be the foreperson of this jury. If that happens, can you lead this jury? Will you be willing and able to do it?" (Mr. Johnson feels a swell of pride: "Me, leading a jury! I'd better straighten my tie.")

This particular strategy probably should be confined to lawyers with weak cases, because if Mr. Johnson doesn't get elected foreperson, you may have increased the likelihood of a hung jury.

Another type of suggestion is about the manner of jury decision. Imagine that a particular attorney wants a quick, emotional decision in the case: a seat-of-the-pants reaction rather than an exacting analysis of the law and the evidence:

> "When the evidence is all in, your presiding juror will tell everyone what the presiding juror thinks your verdict ought to be. Then, the presiding juror will ask the next juror, do you agree with this verdict? And the next one, and so on. And this is the right way to decide a case like this."[19]

This jury speech is designed to get the jurors to decide the case rapidly and superficially, without much discussion, if it works.

But maybe, instead, your theory of the case requires a careful, analytical review of the law and the evidence? "When all the evidence is in, ladies and gentlemen, the presiding juror will guide you through a thorough review of all the evidence and a careful comparing of the evidence to the law."

Collecting Information about the Jurors for Peremptory Challenges. There are many ways to do this. Let's consider a case like *Smith v. Anton* in which you

---

[18] Fed. R. Evid. 609 actually promotes this technical result. The conviction may be used to evaluate Frank Client's credibility, but it cannot be used directly as proof of Frank's propensity to commit the act on trial. Rule 609 expressly limits the use of a conviction "[f]or the purpose of attacking the credibility of a witness." Rule 404 disallows use of such evidence "for the purpose of proving action in conformity therewith."

[19] This idea comes from my father, who was a Professor of Chemical Engineering and became foreperson of a jury. He used this efficient method of deliberation, which was fitting for an engineer, and the jury decided quickly.

represent the defendant, a motorcycle driver who had an accident. Lots of people are wary of motorcycles and consider them unsafe, and you'd like to find that out about these people.

Step One: Paradoxically, Defend the "Wrong" Answer. Use a friend or relative as someone who would give the wrong answer. "My best friend from law school just plain dislikes motorcycles. He thinks they're dangerous, not just to the rider but to everyone else on the road. He really hates 'em. I'm sure you can see, it would be unfair for him to be a juror in this case. What about each of you?"

Step Two: Get Them Ready to Tell You. "Ladies and gentlemen, there are no right or wrong answers. There are only your answers, now, about your honest feelings." "Can you do that, tell what you think, Mr. Firstjuror?" "It's important to dig down into yourself and find your real feelings."

Step Three: Ask the Question, Sympathetically. "So, Mr. Firstjuror, my important question is this. Do you have a thought that you had before you came here, that motorcycles are bad? That they're just too dangerous to be on the road?"

Step Four, Extend the Question to the Whole Panel. "Ms. Green, what would you say about that?" "Mr. Johnson?" "And I expect that there are others who feel like my best friend. If you do, could you please hold up your hand?"

Step Five: Turn the Answer Back Around. After finding out, and perhaps striking some jurors for cause, you have to rehabilitate the "right" answer. "I know everyone can see; it would be unfair to have your mind closed about motorcycles. A lot of nice people ride them. And of course, they're perfectly legal."

Challenges for Cause. The tactics here begin with steps similar to the steps above for peremptory challenges, but you need to really nail down the challenge. If the defense lawyer has found someone who doesn't like motorcycles and seems definite about it, that's probably not enough for a challenge for cause before most judges. The juror isn't yet biased toward a provision of law or against a party. You've got to get them there. Incidentally, it won't work to simply ask, Are you biased? Or prejudiced? Most people don't view themselves as biased or prejudiced. Avoid those words.[20]

Instead, the lawyer asks for a hearing outside the presence of the other

---

[20] This characteristic follows the pattern of cognitive dissonance: the theory that people who find contradictory thoughts in their minds tend to resolve that dissonance, for instance by deciding "I dislike some people because of their ethnicity, but it's right to dislike them, so I'm not biased." See David Crump, *supra* note 4, at 350-52.

jurors, often at the bench, and asks:

> "Ms. Green, it sounds like you just don't like motorcycles. That would be an idea that would follow you all the way through this case, wouldn't it?" "And my side will be representing a person who was riding a motorcycle. It would be impossible for you to keep that out of your mind, and it would shade how you looked at both sides, wouldn't it?"

Next: Force a decision.

> "Ms. Green, the court can't rule on 'maybe.'" "It sounds like you're saying something more like 'yes' than 'no,' isn't that right?" "Now's the time to tell us. This train is leaving the station, and if you're on the jury, you can't get off. It's very unpleasant to be on a jury and find out that you're suddenly unable to do the job."

Finding "Witnesses" among the Jurors (a Rare Tactic). Occasionally, you'll find a potential juror who knows about the place or method that injured your client. I recall a case where the plaintiffs drove their boat right over the dam on a lake and injured themselves badly.

> "Anyone know that place on Lake Hurtyaseff? You do, Mr. Johnson? Is it dangerous? Is it marked so that someone can see it?"

> Answer: "Yes, it's dangerous as heck! You can't see it at all. It's bound to happen that people are going to slide right over it and get hurt real bad."

Now, the other lawyer is jumping up and down, moving for a mistrial. The judge is probably going to just instruct the other people on the panel to disregard it and overrule the motion. You're going to lose that juror to a challenge for cause, but everyone's just heard from the best "witness" ever.

> You don't even know this guy. You haven't gone out and found him. He comes from this precise group, this group of potential jurors. He's one of them.

Injecting Inadmissible Evidence (Don't Do This). It's unethical, of course, and you shouldn't do it. But bad lawyers might, and you have to know all the tactics so you can fight against them.

> "Does anyone work for an insurance agency, like the one that insures Don Defendant in this case?" A marginal lawyer might say that. Object, ask for an instruction to disregard, and move for a mistrial. But the jury has heard it.

A more subtle lawyer might do this: "I'm so glad we have the jury system, and our cases aren't decided by a guy in a tall building in *Omaha,* Nebraska, or *Hartford,* Connecticut."

His hope is that some folks on the jury will figure out that those are insurance company headquarters for Mutual of Omaha and The Hartford Insurance Company. You probably won't do any good by objecting. You'll just call attention to it.

It has to be added: There are legitimate reasons to ask about insurance. Employees are likely to be anti-plaintiff. "Do you, or a relative or friend, work in the insurance industry?" It's not enough for a challenge for cause, but maybe you can zero in and make a stronger case for it. Or you can use a peremptory challenge.[21]

Or, if the jurisdiction prohibits this kind of inquiry, then you say: "Now, you should not base anything about who actually is going to *pay* the judgment that results from this case. Mr. Juror, can you decide the case without considering who is able to, or who is actually going to, pay the judgment?"

NOW, SOME NOTES ABOUT THESE TACTICS

Extreme Diplomacy. This venire contains the jurors that will decide your case. Extreme diplomacy and exaggerated courtesy are called for. Even courtliness. "Ms. Jones, may I be permitted to ask you a few questions?" Don't do this every time, but the first time.

This does not mean that you don't fight for your client. You'll lose their respect and get run over by your opponent. "Ms. Jones, when you say 'I think I can find for the plaintiff if it's proven,' that makes the hair stand up on the back of my neck. Remember, Dan and Meredith are the two most important people in this room to me, and I worry for them. Let me ask it this way: Can you follow the law on that?"

But at all cost, avoid arguing with a member of the panel. If it develops into a disagreement, say, "Thank you, Ms. Jones. You're giving your honest opinion, and I wouldn't want you to act any differently."

---

[21] In Wichmann v. United Disposal, Inc., 553 F.2d 1104 (8th Cir. 1977), the trial judge asked a question similar to this hypothetical example, and the court of appeals approved. (But the appellate court disapproved the judge's further questioning, which addressed the possibility of insurance in the particular case on trial.)

A Smile and a Folksy Manner. At this stage in the trial, your contacts with the jury pool ought usually to be pleasant. Open up with a smile and keep it except when you're describing wrongdoing or injuries. Folksiness helps too. Even quick jokes are okay.

The problem is, you are nervous and anxious during trial, very naturally. Jurors expect you to be relaxed and friendly, which is hard to do. But you've got to be acting a little. Jurors project (unrealistically) that you will be almost neutral in your presentation, clinical and professional. It takes acting on your part.

Once I had a news reporter asking me a ton of questions about a high-profile case right before the jury was to be brought in. I explained that I needed to cut the discussion off and added that I was anxious and nervous about trying the case. Her reaction was clueless. She said, "Nervous? Why?!" She thought I was just part of a game and not concerned with whether the case went my way or not. Jurors are not you. They're more like this news reporter. They're often clueless. They're not like you.

Simple Words. Avoid legalisms. Talk informally. No "therefores" or "learned counsels."

Judge Irving Younger used to do a hilarious bit about a lawyer who would ask, "And what did you do next with respect to the operation and control of your motor vehicle?" To some people, that question is unintelligible—maybe even a distraction. A juror might even think "vehicle" means a passenger bus. Ten questions later, this juror is still puzzling over it. "What does that bus have to do with all this, with the case?"

The question ought, instead, to be simple: "How did you drive your car?" Simple words! Remember that phrases common to law students, like "red herring" and "foundation," may be lost on jurors; you aren't making your point if they're deciphering your legalese.

Legal Limits and Ethics. The suggestions above probably contain material that would not be proper in some states. Know what is proper and know what kinds of statements will get the judge to come down on you with the voice of thunder.

Come Out "Smoking Hot." My friend Murry Cohen used this description. Your beginning should hit hard. Sharp words; placing blame. Murry said this in connection with appellate arguments. I think it is good advice in a jury trial too.

Always Have a Question Ready. Whatever you are talking about, have a question ready for jurors about the subject. The purpose of voir dire is not to give long speeches. That's for opening statement and final argument. Many courts will interrupt you if you go on for more than four or five sentences as background for a question. Naturally, you've got to tell the jurors some information so that they can understand your questions, but always have a question ready.

WHAT WOULD AN OUTLINE OF THE VOIR DIRE LOOK LIKE?

This is probably the hardest phase of trial to outline because you have to interact with the jurors, and you may have to shift among your subjects to keep up with them. This outline is only one of many ways to do it.

I. I'm David Garrison. Solo practitioner.
> Mr. Oswald Opposition, on other side, with Dewey Cheatum & Howe.
> More than 400 lawyers. Anyone know any?
> I Represent Meredith and Daniel Smith
> Most important people in courtroom. Stand up, Meredith and Dan.

II. Thank you, jurors. Civic Responsibility and Honor. Part of backbone of America.

III. We are here because daughter Sarah, 6 years old, was killed by a motorcycle driven by John Anton [point at him] at way past speed limit, 50 to 65 mph, at 3:15 in a school zone, 20-mph limit. Law says gross negligence. *[Come out smoking hot.]*
> Three Themes: 1. Describe Anton's conduct. Grossly negligent.
> 2. They will try to blame the deceased child. Outrageous. She acted normally.
> 3. It will take over $ 10 million . . .

IV. Anybody know anyone here or at Dewey firm?

V. This is a negligence case.
> I expect Judge Thompson will tell you what negligence is . . . [read the pattern definition]
> That's a lot of words. Really, negligence means "carelessness"
> Ms. Jones, can you decide whether there is negligence—carelessness?
> [Or: Whether someone was guilty of an unreasonable act?]
> *[Discussing the law so as to lower the standard.]*

VI. Civil case: a "preponderance of evidence"
> Just means greater weight

Illustrate with arms out both sides: Imagine scales of justice

If it tips slightly, that's greater weight. Ms. Green, can you follow this rule?

Not like across street in criminal courts: higher burden because loss of freedom.

VII. I expect defendant will blame little Sarah, saying she was negligent

Different standard for child: a child of same age & ability

Sarah just doing what usual child would do

Ms. Green, can you apply this more lenient standard to little Sarah when they try to blame her? *[Discussing law to lower standard]*

VIII. I have to tell you, Mr. Opposition may bring it out, I hope he doesn't . . .

Little Sarah didn't cross street in crosswalk but a few feet outside

But you will see: it had absolutely nothing to do with her death. She's a child. Cause is Anton. *[Inoculation]*

IX. Law says one witness is enough to prove a point if you believe that witness

Can you follow the law?

I should add we will have much more than one witness.

[Conditioning jurors to accept your proof.]

X. We will bring you all evidence we know.

I hope Mr. Opponent will be doing the same.

[Conditioning jurors]

XI. I expect at the end to be telling you that damages greater than $ 10 million

All we have in court is compensation, dollars

Does it sound like too much money, Ms. Green, for loss of daughter . . . because of grossly negligent defendant, if proven?

We will have evidence, including Professor Noddingly, economist.

[Conditioning jurors]

XII. [If a juror seems unfavorable and may turn out to be struck:]

My sister Kathy thinks money damages shouldn't be permitted. I love her, of course, but she shouldn't be on this jury.

Does anyone here agree with Kathy? Or think damages too high?

Ms. Cratchit, you held hand up. Will we start out in your mind ten yards back in this race when we ask for money damages like I've said?

Now, the judge can't rule on Maybe. It sounds like the answer is more No than Yes. *[Setting up for a Challenge for Cause.]*

XIII. Momentarily I will sit down. Mr. Opposition will talk to you. Law says, what he tells you is not evidence. Can you promise me—and promise Dan and Meredith—that you will wait until we present our case?

WHICH POTENTIAL JURORS DO YOU STRIKE?

This is an Impossible Question to Answer. There are no clear or universal strategies. The basic idea is that you want to remove jurors who will not view your case favorably. In other words, you strike the ones who will be against you. Sometimes people forget that, in an effort to fit into some potential rule or other.

So, how do you choose the jurors who are against you?

The Only Workable General Rule I Know Of is based on how different people make decisions. It's my distillation of experiences in the school of hard knocks. Here it is:

> In every case, there is one side (Side 1) that will benefit from having jurors who will decide emotionally and an opposing side (Side 2) that will benefit from having jurors who will make a hard analysis of the facts and the law. See which side you are on and strike accordingly.

In our model case here, *Smith v. Anton,* the Smiths, who are plaintiffs, are likely to be Side 1, the side that benefits from a more emotional approach. Plaintiff likes people pleasers, those who work in sales and the like. Defendant Anton, then, is Side 2, wanting a hard analysis of the law and facts. Defendant would like a bank loan officer who says "No" to loan applications or a geologist who says, "Drill here." Plaintiff strikes bankers, managers, and the like, and wants shoe salesmen. Defendant strikes beauticians or shoe salesmen and prefers bankers.

But even this idea has to give way to other considerations. Imagine that a banker on the panel is just like the plaintiff in education and personality and answers questions emotionally and favorably to the plaintiff's side. This guy or woman might be less subject to being stricken than a beautician who has a higher education and doesn't answer favorably to the plaintiff's side.

How do you decide whom to strike, then? Plaintiff's lawyer (Side 1) wants jurors who are people pleasers in their occupations. Beauticians, salespeople, waiters. They don't regularly make analytically based decisions and are more likely to decide morally or emotionally. The defense (Side 2) wants people who make difficult decisions in their occupations from limited data. Loan officers, administrators, geologists. A geologist, for example, studies all the available data, indicates a point on a chart, and says, "Drill here." A hard analysis.

Side 1 will strike the jurors that Side 2 wants. And Side 2 will strike the jurors that Side 1 wants. In the ambiguous atmosphere of a voir dire in a courtroom, this approach is unavoidably mushy—and imperfect.

Aside from that, the so-called rules are less useful.

I remember the so-called "P rule," which was said to apply in criminal cases. As an assistant district attorney, if I followed the P rule (although I didn't), I would strike potential jurors whose occupations began with the letter P. I would strike plumbers, psychologists, philosophers, and part-time anyone. The trouble was, you could use a synonym and change the outcome of the P rule. A "student" could be called a "pupil," and this way the person's job would begin with a P, and I was supposed to vanish that person. Also, there was a bigger problem, the problem that the P rule—well, it just didn't work.

The Similarity Rule. A lot of people instinctively go by a rule in which someone similar to the party you represent is a preferable juror. Maybe— sometimes. This rule would tell you to choose women if you are prosecuting a rape case. Women are, certainly, similar to women who are survivors of rape. Trouble is, I found that women in rape cases can be unsympathetic to other women.

Why? The answer requires guesswork. I'm guessing that it reflects a phenomenon that psychologists call "cognitive dissonance."

Is There a Cognitive Dissonance Rule? This odd result—women biased against women—is likely at least partially to be what the psychologists call a "dissonance" phenomenon. What's that? When we have two conflicting thoughts in our brains, we unconsciously try to get rid of the dissonance this situation causes. This is the theory of "cognitive dissonance," pioneered by psychologist Leon Festinger. And so, for example, turncoat witnesses, who once despised "snitches," begin to believe that helping law enforcement is noble, when they testify against their former associates. (Snitching is bad, but now I'm a snitch. My mind will reduce the dissonance by telling me I'm doing the right thing.).

How Does Dissonance Affect Jurors? Here's how. A juror looks at the situation of a plaintiff who is horribly injured by the negligence of another person and thinks, "That could happen to anyone. It could happen to me! No no no!" And of course, the juror doesn't want that—doesn't want to suffer the same injuries; doesn't even want to think about or visualize that. It could happen to me, but it just can't happen to me. And that is the dissonance.

The juror's mind finds ways to reduce the dissonance. The mind reasons that

"It really couldn't, or wouldn't, happen to *me.*" The juror unconsciously thinks, "I would have driven more slowly." "I would have braked earlier." "I wouldn't have been on that dangerous street in the first place." And—"Therefore, this terrible kind of accident wouldn't happen to me." The plaintiff is different from me and acted differently. "The plaintiff became a victim because she made the wrong choices"—the route she drove, the speed she was going, etc. It was "actually the plaintiff who was negligent here."

This phenomenon is real. Psychologists have conducted experiments and found, repeatedly, that people are biased against the victims of accidents or crimes.

And so, if you can find those people, the ones who are probably siding against victims of accidents from the beginning and before hearing any evidence, you know whom to strike, if you are the plaintiff, and whom to keep, if you are the defendant. Trial lawyers who can do this are very successful. The trouble is, it's hard to get this kind of information during voir dire.

And so, the question, "Whom do I strike?" is impossible to answer clearly or in a general way.

Chapter 3

OPENING STATEMENT

THE LAW GOVERNING OPENING STATEMENT

Some courts are very strict about the law of opening statement. It's supposed to cover only your theory of the case and your evidence. It's not supposed to include any argument. Some judges will react negatively even to statements like "cold-blooded murderer."[22] But others say that a lawyer is to have "great latitude."[23] The Supreme Court has said that the "narrow purpose" of an opening statement is to "state what evidence will be presented, to make it easier for the jurors to understand what is to follow, and to relate parts of the evidence and testimony to the whole; it is not an occasion for argument."[24]

The mock opening statement that follows takes some "latitude," but not too much, it is to be hoped; you will have to consider your jurisdiction and the court trying your case.

THE CASE WE ARE USING[25]

This opening statement is based on the same model case we have been using in this book:

Plaintiffs Daniel and Meredith Smith are suing John Anton. The plaintiffs' witnesses say that Anton drove his motorcycle in a school zone at 3:15 p.m. at speeds estimated at 50 to 65 mph by a police officer, Officer Hauseshorn, and by Meredith Smith. He collided with little Sarah Smith, their six-year-old daughter, and killed her while she was walking home from school. They have an economist and themselves to testify to damages, which they claim

---

[22] Lawrence v. Superintendent Dallas SCI, 849 Fed. Appx. 386, 387 (3d Cir. 2021).

[23] Wright v. Barr, 62 S.W.3d 509, 532-33 (Mo. App. 2001).

[24] Arizona v. Washington, 434 U.S. 497, 513 & n.2, 517 (1978).

[25] This statement also appears in an article on *Opening Statements* by this author.

exceed $ 10 million.

Anton's defense includes a witness who followed him and Anton himself, who will testify that he was going slowly, under the 20-mph speed limit. The child darted into the street and he couldn't stop. The defense also says that the damages claim is very exaggerated.

THE OPENING STATEMENT MIGHT SOUND LIKE THIS

"Good morning, ladies and gentlemen of the jury. I am David Garrison, and I represent Meredith and Daniel Smith.

[Only if you haven't already thanked the jurors:] "I'd like to thank you for being here to do your civic duty by serving on a jury. It's a job that only free people can perform.[26]

"Now, in this trial, I, on the plaintiffs' side, will represent Meredith and Daniel Smith. Stand up for a moment, Meredith and Daniel. Now, ladies and gentlemen of the jury, these two are the most important people in the courtroom for me. [Only if you haven't done this in voir dire.]

"They have endured a loss that is hard to feel unless someone is in their position, and I hope everyone present never is. They have lost their beautiful daughter Sarah, just six years old, due to the negligence [pointing] of this man sitting here, John Anton, the defendant.

"We will have witnesses to show you three themes about this case. Here they are:

"Our first theme is that John Anton drove his motorcycle not just too fast, but way too fast, through a group of children going home from school at 3:15 p.m. in the afternoon in a school zone. He was negligent; in fact, he was grossly negligent. The judge will tell you about negligence, but in essence, here it is: negligence is just 'carelessness.' And John Anton showed a lot of carelessness that awful day.[27]

"Second, we will show you that the defendant's effort to claim that Sarah, little Sarah, was contributorily negligent is bogus. They blame her for her own death. Given the evidence, that is a just plain awful argument.

---

[26] Is this comment within the allowed purpose of an opening statement in your jurisdiction?
[27] Is this "translation" of the law appropriate in your jurisdiction?

"Third, we will show you that it would take more than ten million dollars to compensate for this terrifying loss. You can't bring Sarah back. Our court system can only award money to 'compensate' the survivors. And if someone suffers this kind of loss, what amount in dollars is enough to compensate them?

"And we will have some very strong witnesses to prove these facts.

"Our first witness will be Deputy Sheriff Milton Hauseshorn. He was the officer who came onto the scene first. He interviewed witnesses, including children. He took measurements. He estimates the speed of John Anton's motorcycle at 55 to 65 miles per hour, when the speed limit was 20 miles an hour. John Anton knocked the body of this poor child a hundred and five feet. A third of a football field. There were blood spots at three different places, sort of like a stone skipping over the water. Officer Hauseshorn's conclusion is clear. He is certain that John Anton was negligent, and that John Anton caused this child's death.

"Our next witnesses will be two of the children who saw the whole thing. They will tell you that little Sarah was not contributorily negligent. She did not cause her own death. She just did what all the other children did in crossing the street right after school let out. The judge will tell you that the negligence of a child is different. Instead of adult carelessness, it's based on what a six-year-old child would do.[28]

"Next, Meredith Smith will tell you what she saw. She is Sarah's mother, and she was in her back yard. She saw the motorcycle and her estimate is that it was going over 50 miles per hour. So, you have two independent witnesses giving you similar estimates: that the motorcycle was going more than twice the speed limit. Meredith, whom you see right here, ran out and cradled her own child's bloody body, lying in the street. Sarah died in her arms.

"Next, we will call Dr. Mark Cezyck, who is the Medical Examiner in this county, similar to a 'coroner.' He will tell you precisely about the injuries inflicted on little Sarah and the causes of her death.

"Then, we will call Professor James Noddingly. He is a labor economist. He will tell you about the tremendous costs of hiring a child actor to perform all the little tasks of a child like Sarah, six years old. It's not replacing Sarah, of course. This is a common method of proving what the death of a child can be compensated by, even if it doesn't show the exact thing.

---

[28] Again, is this treatment of the law appropriate?

"Finally, Daniel and Meredith will tell you about dozens of little events they had with their daughter. Daniel remembers, for example, the excitement he and little Sarah felt when they decorated the Christmas tree last year—last year, and for the last time. And Meredith will tell you about other events too.

"And both of them will tell you their plans and visions of the future with Sarah—her days in school, the next grade, and on to her graduation from college and walking her down the aisle. All of it is lost due to John Anton's negligence. And you will be able to see why I say it would take more than ten million dollars to compensate for such a loss.

"Thank you again, ladies and gentlemen. I know you will do the right thing."

NOW, WHAT WILL YOUR OUTLINE OF AN
OPENING STATEMENT LOOK LIKE?

I. I am David Garrison, solo practitioner.

    Mr. Oswald Opposition . . . from Dewey Cheatum & Howe . . . More than 400 lawyers [if not already said to jury]

II. We will show you three themes:

    1. Daughter Sarah, six years old, killed by motorcycle driven by John Anton not just too fast, but *way* too fast, 50 to 65 mph in a school zone at 3:15 when children walking home, 20 mph school zone. Gross negligence.

    2. They will attempt to blame little Sarah for her death, saying contributorily negligent. Frankly, that's an awful argument. Remember child's lenient standard for child negligence. Sarah just acted like normal 6-year-old. That's why we have school zones in the first place.

    3. It would take more than 10 million dollars to compensate for Dan and Meredith's loss. It is an enormous loss, too big for anyone to understand unless it happens to you (and I hope not, to you, ever).

III. Our first witness: First, we will call Deputy Sheriff Milton Hauseshorn. He will tell you that he made the scene at 3:30. He measured everything and did calculations. And he will tell you that John Anton drove his motorcycle at 55 to 65 mph. Officer Hauseshorn is an expert witness, and he has both the education and the experience to back that up.

IV. We will also call Meredith Smith, who is little Sarah's mother. She saw John Anton driving his motorcycle and killing her daughter. Her estimate is that John Anton was going 50 to 60 mph. So, you see, we'll have two independent witnesses whose speeds overlap.

V. We will call Dr. Mark Cezyck, Medical Examiner. He will tell you that he performed an autopsy on the body of little Sarah. He will tell you that she had eggshell fracturing of the skull, and terrible bruises all over, and a compound fracture of the tibia with the bone sticking out at an almost right angle, and all kinds of internal injuries. He too is a very expert witness.

VI.   Then, we will call Dr. James Noddingly. He is a professor of economics. He will help you to estimate the damages to Meredith and Daniel Smith and help show why damages will be over $ 10 million.

VII. We will also hear again from Daniel and Meredith on damages. They will tell you about their life with little Sarah. They will talk about all the times they remember about their baby girl. Daniel will tell about putting ornaments on the Christmas tree and how excited they both were. And they will tell about their hopes for Sarah in the future: graduating from elementary school and high school, her job, her marriage, walking her down the aisle.

Chapter 4

PRESENTING THE EVIDENCE

DIRECT EXAMINATION: THE PROBLEMS

Let's Start with Direct Examination. That's what usually starts a trial. It's the way you prove something, if you have the burden of proof.

Direct Is Actually Harder than Cross. It's worth setting out the reasons for its difficulty, because the techniques we're going to look at in this chapter are better understood then. So, what are the problems?

1. Direct Examination Means You've Called This Witness, and the Jury Expects You to Prove Something. You don't get to choose all of your witnesses. You especially don't get to choose your major witnesses. The jurors sit and look at you and the witnesses. Jury expectations are that you have called this witness, and they expect you to show them something. I've heard people tell me, "It's just like watching TV." I believe it. They want to lie back and hear an interesting story.

2. Your Witnesses May Not Be Good Storytellers, but That's What It Takes. The ordinary person isn't good at telling a story. Most people talk in disorganized bits, and they have to go back and fill the story in. They don't all come with a flair for the dramatic. But that's what you need.

3. The Rules of Evidence Limit How Much Guidance You Can Give to Witnesses. The Rules say you can't lead on direct except in a few circumstances. If you try to help a witness, your opponent will stand up and object, "Leading Question." You'll have to learn techniques for getting around this problem.

4. Many Witnesses Are Nervous—or Even Scared to Death. If you're Meredith Smith in our model case, you've probably never seen the inside of a courtroom. You feel isolated. Everyone's looking at you. Everyone—including you, the attorney, the opposing attorney, the judge, the clerk, the bailiff, twelve jurors, spectators—and a killer, as she sees him.

5. The Tactics of Cross Examination Can Be Cheap and Easy by Comparison. Sometimes a lawyer can ridicule your witness with just a couple of questions. Other times, the lawyer might cross-examine your witness for many hours, looking for weariness and mistakes.

6. The Other Side Has Different and Unaccustomed Ways of Sizing Up the Evidence. If you're Meredith Smith, you can expect to be asked, "Why didn't you walk Sarah to and from school?" "Why did Sarah jaywalk? You didn't teach her not to?" This set of questions is not part of Meredith's thinking pattern.

7. We Lawyers Sometimes Talk with Fancy Words. I've already addressed this issue in an earlier chapter. It applies with witness questioning too. We use 50-cent words when we should be using 5-cent words. For example, I had a habit of using the words "previously" and "subsequently." The trouble was, a lot of witnesses don't understand those words, or worse, they think that they each mean the opposite of what they mean. One day when I was addressing a witness with these words and she didn't understand me, the judge interrupted and said, "Use before and after." I did, and the examination went well.

8. Many Legal Standards Depend Not on a Single Question but on the Mood of the Entire Body of Evidence and Argument. In *Smith v. Anton,* our model case, the key legal question is negligence. But negligence doesn't depend on one fact. Or one participant's actions. Or one witness. It depends on all the facts—everything throughout the trial.

It depends on the *mood* you create about the defendant's actions. Think about a scary movie, those movies that come on television a few weeks before Halloween. The scriptwriter and the director have worked hard to create a scary mood, a scary scene, and all kinds of scary moments. That's what you've got to do in proving negligence.

SO, WHAT TECHNIQUES PRODUCE A GOOD DIRECT EXAMINATION?

Here are some tactics that have come to me via the school of hard knocks.

Chronological Order. People absorb information poorly if it's only through their ears. So, go through the evidence chronologically. It's hard to do. We don't usually talk this way in ordinary conversation. "This happened . . . that happened . . . and before this happened, the other thing happened . . . ." That jumbled sequence is deadly for jury understanding. Instead, your organization is chronological. There are times to use different organizations—sometimes, item by item, and sometimes expert witnesses—but for the ordinary witness, be rigorously chronological.

What if the witness gets off track and talks about an event out of order? Remember, you're the captain of this ship. You are responsible for getting the witness back in sequence. Redirect the witness.

These ideas are not to be found in the Rules of Evidence. But I've never had an objection to them. For one thing, it's usually too quick to invite an objection.

Non-Leading Formulas. The rule against leading questions on direct is a cause for frustration. Your opponent loves objecting on this basis if the judge sustains him or her. The problem is, a non-leading question doesn't suggest the answer, and it often doesn't suggest what the question is about, either.

I recall a counterfeiting case where I was appointed on appeal. I laughed out loud reading the record. The Assistant U.S. Attorney asked, "What did you see when you came into the room?" The cooperating witness answered, "There was this calendar tacked to the wall with this sexy lady and all she had on was . . . ." The AUSA backed up a bit and asked, "Was there anything in the room that was unusual?" The witness said, "Nothing unusual that I saw." The AUSA finally gave up and said, "Was there any counterfeit money on the table or anything?"

These guys, the defendants, they didn't think a stash of counterfeit was unusual.

Anyway, here are some non-leading formulas:

State the facts as to whether . . .: "State the facts as to whether there was any counterfeit money on the table."
Anything unusual? This one can still work. "Was there anything unusual on the table?"
Multiple choice. "Was it ___, or was it ___?" "Were the robbers just kind of loafing along, or were they really hauling it?"

Directing your attention. "Directing your attention to the table, what did you see on it?" Clumsy but functional. A dangling modifier that works fine.

Another Technique: Signposting—Letting the Jury Know Where You're Going. Again, people take information poorly when it's only through their ears. It's easy to lose the jury's ability to follow you. So, you tell the jury about every change of scene beforehand. I call it "signposting": giving a signal to the witness and the jury when you're changing or doing something technical.

"Now, Mr. Witness, I want to take you from the accident scene to the hospital and what happened there." Or, "Mr. Witness, I'm going to ask you some questions about this document, Exhibit 34. These are questions that are required by the Rules of Evidence. . . . "First, is Exhibit 34 the kind of document that originates with someone with personal knowledge of the events it records?"

Without the introduction, jurors might think you've taken leave of your senses. The question sounds weird if you haven't been to law school. When you finish the business record predicate, you say something like, "Now, I want to get back to your testimony about the accident."

Symbolic Detail. Sometimes, there's a piece of information that symbolizes your theory of the case even though it's not particularly strong proof of it. I recall a little incident that I made into a major event in my negligent homicide case, from which our model case in this book is taken: the motorcycle rider who took the life of little Sarah.

Sarah's father, Daniel Smith, came home from work after the accident. He walked up and down the street. I almost think he hoped he might find Sarah, alive and well. Instead, he found her glasses. They were in two pieces, with one of the lenses on one side of the street and the rest on the other side.

I got him to describe this event. I put the two parts into evidence, marked as two different exhibits. I even laid them out in the courtroom, approximately apart the same distance as they were on two sides of the street. The inference was that the motorcycle had knocked them that far apart.

It wasn't powerful evidence in a logical sense. But it was symbolic detail. It symbolized the size and power of the motorcycle in comparison to the helplessness of the tiny child.

There is symbolic detail in every case—even breach-of-contract cases, even antitrust cases. Find it and make a big deal out of it.

Visual Aids and Evidence. From what I've said earlier, you can infer what I'm going to say about this. "Real" evidence—the gun that killed the victim, the crumpled fender of a car—is more impressive than description. If you can't produce that, a sharp photograph, blown up in size, is almost as good. And then too, I have always believed in charts, graphs, diagrams. When I was an Assistant DA, I had a case with a car made up of parts of a green car, a red car, and a blue car. I made my own diagram by hand with markers of the three colors. It probably could have been done by testimony alone, but the diagram worked better, even hand drawn by that fine artist, me.

Euphonious, Partisan Rhetoric. Choose words that advance your case. If the accident was caused by a drunk driver who took an intoxilyzer test, and you represent the injured plaintiffs, you should call the device an "instrument" and ask about the use of its methods in the space program. But if you are the defense lawyer, it's a "machine" or even a "gizmo," and you ask, "How often do you change the sprockets and gears and rubber bands inside that gizmo?" There aren't any, but the question works.

I know a skillful trial lawyer who advised plaintiff's lawyers in medical malpractice cases not to use the word "medical." The reason? Everyone is sympathetic to doctors who get sued over and over again in those awful, unfair medical malpractice cases.

And don't adopt your opponent's rhetoric unless it helps your case. If the opponent calls the device considered above a "machine," you shouldn't echo that term out of laziness. (It's easy to do.) Stick to calling it an "instrument." But if the defense lawyer refers to the "parade of horrors we had in developing this MRI," you can adopt this phrase, "parade of horrors" and hang it on the other side several times.

A PATTERN FOR TESTIMONY FROM A FACT WITNESS

Like most of the chapters in this book, this technique comes from the school of hard knocks, my most effective teacher.

Step 1: Name. "What is your name?" Easy. Something to start with, that doesn't take much effort. Or if you want to be a little fancier, "Please introduce yourself to the jury by telling them your name."

Step 2: The Orientation Question. I bet you haven't heard about this idea. Here, make a short, leading question that tells the jury who this witness is. "Officer Hauseshorn, you are the deputy sheriff who made the scene and investigated it, is that right?" Ask a similar orientation question of all your witnesses.

Why ask this question? Because you want to avoid jury confusion. Because it helps to orient the jury. Some jurors may otherwise think that this is an officer who made an arrest in this case, and as a result, they miss the first ten questions and answers. Another example: "You are little Sarah's mother, and you're here to tell the jury what you saw happen to her?"

Although it's a leading question, it's background. Short and introductory. Background leading is permitted. I never got an objection. Also, it sounds like a professional way to begin things.

Step 3: Witness Background. For the plaintiff or other major witnesses, this part should be carefully drawn. "Do you live here, in Springfield?" "Did you grow up here?" "What high school?" "I went to Waltrip High School." (That's a school in my city.)

This may turn out to be an important connection. If someone on the jury went to Waltrip High School, played football against Waltrip, or maybe even just knows about Waltrip, the witness is made more familiar. And familiarity, psychologists say, is one of the few ingredients of attraction. You've enhanced the attractiveness of your witness—and your case.

Don't stop there. Family? Kids? What kind of work? Even hobbies. I once asked a police officer, "Do you have any hobbies?" His answer: "Yes. I collect guns and shoot rattlers." My reaction was, "Whoo. I shouldn't have asked that." But at the end, I got a good result. I noticed that one of the jurors went over to talk to the officer. He had a ponytail at a time when ponytails on men were not yet fashionable, and he had a white T-shirt with a picture of an upraised fist. I figured he was going to tell the officer an earful about PO-Leece brutality. But instead, the two of them were talking excitedly about—you guessed it—collecting guns and shooting rattlers.

Step 4: "Directing Your Attention" to the Inciting Event. You begin the real testimony this way: "Directing your attention to the date, August 10 of last year, did you have occasion to be driving on the East Freeway?" Your English teacher would be horrified. (Can you see why? "Directing your attention" is a dangling modifier! Remember??) But your English teacher only taught you how to write an essay and forgot to mention that there are many ways of communicating.

"Directing your attention" is lawyer talk. But that's okay; you're a lawyer. It signals to the witness and to the jury that you're now going to be talking about the meat of the coconut, so to speak. It's signposting.

Step 5: Chronologically, Strictly Chronologically, develop the story. It's not easy to do. As I said above, it's not the way people normally talk. But a here-and-there style, a looping kind of sequence, might be deadly in front of a jury, because—again—people take in information poorly through their ears alone.

What if you yourself get things out of order? Then you've got to backtrack. Make sure the jury has a clear understanding of the order of things.

So, it sounds more professional, and it enhances jury understanding, if you rigorously stick to chronological order.

Step 6: Tell the Jury When You Switch Subjects. "Now, Ms. Witness, I want to take you away from the accident scene to the hospital, when you saw your little girl Sarah there." Signposting, again. If you don't do this, you may find that jurors miss several questions and answers because they didn't know who this witness was.

Step 7: "I Pass the Witness." Say this at the end.

BUT AN EXPERT WITNESS IS DIFFERENT

In our model case, *Smith v. Anton,* plaintiff will call two expert witnesses: Deputy Sheriff Milton Hauseshorn and Economist James Q. Noddingly. Let's take the economist first, because his testimony is that of a traditional expert.

This isn't about the *Daubert*-type issue or whatever the test for expert opinions is in your state. We assume, here, that you've already qualified the expert in a *Daubert* hearing. The issue is how to present the expert's opinion to the jury.

Step 1: Name. Just as before.

Step 2: Orientation Question, just as before. "Professor Noddingly, you're an economist, and you're here to help the jury with the plaintiff's damages in this case, is that right?"

Step 3: Cover the Issue of the Expert's Fee Yourself. "Doctor Noddingly, I assume that, like most expert witnesses, you've charged your usual fee, by the hour?" "And what is the total amount, as of now?" "And it doesn't depend on the outcome of this case, or what the jury does, does it?"

You know that the opponent is going to bring this out. You can make it sound normal. It's inoculation.

Step 4: Thoroughly Bring Out the Expert's Qualifications. Education: college, post-college, doctorate. Thesis. Awards or accomplishments. Publications and presentations. Fields of study. Consulting and contracting events for private and government agencies (name them all and tell what they do). Take time to build the expert's credentials.

Step 5: Ask for the Expert's Opinion. "Dr. Noddingly, did you develop opinions about the value, as seen by an economist, of a child to her mom and dad, Daniel and Meredith?" "Yes, I did." "And what is that valuation?" "It would take more than ten million dollars in compensation for the death of this child Sarah."

The rules let you do this—ask for the opinion before explaining how it was developed—and it has several advantages, which we'll describe in a moment.

Step 6: Ask for the Methods behind the Opinion. This is going to be complex. It will include the idea of a shadow market: "Doctor, would you explain what a shadow market is?" "When we have to value something that has no clear dollar price, we use a shadow market. We try to measure something else that will give us a measure of the thing without a dollar cost. For example, the EPA has to place a value on the price of a human life. They look to the premium in wages for a dangerous job over a lifetime, and it turns out to be $ 10.5 million dollars. $ 10.5 million."

The expert proceeds to tell the jury the cost in dollars of hiring a child actor to interact with the parents through growing up and through life events. He also explains why this shadow market fits. "Is it the same as having Sarah?" "No, of course not. But all the courts can do is compensation."

And the expert performs several mathematical calculations, culminating in reducing the sum to present value. "So, this is compensation for the death of Sarah, if paid now in cash." Which is the answer the jury must give to the damages question. It is the same as the opinion given earlier.

Step 7: Repeat the Opinion. "So, Professor Noddingly, what is your opinion about the compensation owed to Daniel and Meredith Smith?" And the jury hears it again.

"Isn't it kind of an economic and bloodless way to value a human tragedy?" "Yes, but all we have in the courts is money compensation."

What are the advantages of this order of presentation, with the opinion given first, before the explanation? There will be some who are unable to follow the explanation. They have the opinion first, and they can tune out during the explanation. For those who follow the explanation, having the opinion first is helpful to their understanding of the explanation. You do get the opinion fully developed, of course. And you can repeat the opinion again at the end.

Step 8: Thank you, Dr. Noddingly. I pass the witness.

Step 9: Watch the Cross Examination Carefully. Don't just sit there. Be ready to object forcefully. And take notes for your redirect examination.

EFFECTIVE CROSS EXAMINATION

This Is the Flip Side, so to Speak, of Direct Examination. And like direct examination, it can be successfully done with some basic techniques. But the tactics are different from those for direct examination.

Cross examination is not limited in the same way as direct. You can lead. And the conventional wisdom says that if you're a beginner, *every* question should be a leading question. Only a veteran cross-examiner can depart from this rule with impunity.

Judge Irving Younger was the past master of this subject. His "Ten Commandments of Cross Examination" is a classic. I don't agree with all of it. For example, Younger says, "Be prepared," but that's universal advice, and "Be brief," but there are times when it's wiser to examine the witness at length. And he says, "Save for summation," but I say, don't save it (instead, develop it both in evidence and in argument), and he says "Listen," but again, that's universal. These four "commandments" aren't helpful.

Younger's work remains a classic. My coverage of this subject has some relationship to his. In each instance, I have a different take on the subject because of my study in the school of hard knocks.

MY TEN PRINCIPLES OF CROSS EXAMINATION

So, here are some principles of good cross examination. My own "Ten Principles of Cross Examination," maybe, which has ideas that resemble parts of Irving Younger's classic but are different.

1. Don't Repeat the Direct Examination. Inexperienced lawyers, who don't know what to ask, sometimes "fill in" with questions that will repeat what was said on direct. "So, Professor Noddingly, you used a shadow market?" "And what did that tell you?" "And you concluded that the damages were $ 10 million?"[29]

The jury's heard it once. Give it to them a second time by *your* examination, and they're sure to believe it—to believe your opponent's version of the case, that is.

2. Don't Beat Up the Other Side's Victims. If you represent the plaintiffs and if John Anton's mother happens to testify, realize that she is a victim too. Her son is in trouble, and she's tormented about it. Don't give her a bad time; the jury won't like it.

3. Don't Invite Witness Explanation. It's easy to make this mistake. But don't, for goodness's sake. This mistake comes up when you've just gotten the witness to say something that sounds wrong to you. So, you're tempted to ask, "How can you possibly say that?"

You've now invited the witness to give an explanation—the witness's explanation. And the witness proceeds to explain, in a plausible way. And all you can do is sit and listen, along with the jury. And you think to yourself, "Gee, his

---

[29] This idea loosely resembles one of Irving Younger's commandments.

answer is perjurious. But I bet the jury buys it." Don't invite the witness to give an explanation because it's practically certain that the witness will get up on a soap box (figuratively) and deliver a speech against you.[30]

4. Use Only Leading Questions (Unless You Are Sure of a Helpful Answer). You're permitted to use leading questions. It's in the Rules. And the conventional wisdom is that *every* question should be a leading question.[31]

In other words, you should be asking, "It was raining really hard outside, wasn't it?" rather than saying, "What was the weather outside?" The second of these questions invites the witness to talk in an open-ended way, and the answer may surprise you—and hurt you. The leading question is better because it centers the witness on your theory of the case.

A leading question, in the language of the Rules, is one that "suggests" the answer. "It was raining hard outside, wasn't it?" suggests the answer; in fact, it zeroes in on the answer. You'd like to have the witness saying "Yes," "Yes," "Yes" to your sequence of leading questions.

But Patrick A. Malone, in his book "The Fearless Cross-Examiner," disagrees with the conventional wisdom about leading questions. He says that it is possible to ask questions in cross examination so that the witness gives answers that support your goals in the case. This method works, he explains, if the cross examiner is fearless.

I think he is on to something, and I think he's right in saying that the answer on cross is more persuasive if it comes from the witness rather than from you. But I think Mr. Malone's advice is most helpful if it is directed at lawyers with some significant trial experience. For a beginner, I'd advise using the leading-question-only approach. If you're certain that the witness will give the answer you want to a non-leading question, you might chance it—or not.[32]

5. Don't Adopt Your Opponent's Terminology (Unless It Helps Your Case). I've already introduced this idea. If you want to introduce results from an intoxilyzer test to prove that someone was under the influence, you may notice that your opponent calls the device a "machine" or a "gizmo." But you shouldn't. You

---

[30] This idea loosely resembles one of Irving Younger's commandments.
[31] This idea, too, loosely resembles one of Younger's commandments. If someone is telling about a technique or tactic, it is likely to resemble others' descriptions in at least some aspects.
[32] This idea comes from one of Younger's commandments too.

should use your own terminology, because your opponent has different purposes. You should refer to the intoxilyzer as an "instrument."

But if your opponent happens to blurt out, "The intoxilyzer is an accurate instrument," that's different (this sort of thing happens sometimes). Use your opponent's words. You can work several references to "this accurate instrument" into your handling of the case from now on.

6. Don't Argue with the Witness. You'll lose with the jury if you do. You're a fancy lawyer, and the witness usually is not. How should you handle it? An example: You—"Officer Hauseshorn didn't say *that,* did he?" The witness—"He certainly did!" You—"Well, we'll have to trust the jury to remember it correctly." And immediately, you proceed to your next question.

If it's a crucial point, you may have to do something more, such as recalling the officer. But don't try to solve the problem by arguing with the witness.

7. Simple Words. We've covered this point, but it's particularly important in cross examination. Use "before" and "after" rather than "previous" and "subsequent."

8. Don't Try to Destroy the Witness. Knocking down the witness's credibility a little—that should usually be your goal, rather than complete destruction. Unless it's absolutely clear that the witness is a complete liar, you shouldn't overdo the effort. Juries are forgiving. They don't usually discard the witness's testimony completely because of one impeachment or contradiction.

9. Read All of the Witness's Statements or Depositions in the Case Beforehand. Lawyers are constantly in a hurry, constantly overloaded. It is understandable if they try to avoid work that may not turn out to be necessary. It's a survival instinct.

But I tried always to go into trial having read or reread all of the witness material. (Notice my words: I "tried.") It is tempting to think, this guy will be a bad witness, and I can handle him without overdoing the reading. But don't. If the case settles on the courtroom steps, you'll be ready in your mind and you'll negotiate more effectively.

10. Outline the Cross Examination Beforehand. I did this with the other sides' major witnesses. You don't know how the cross examination is going to go, of course, and you need maximum flexibility. But an outline won't interfere with that. Unless, that is, you write out all your questions. That's unwise. An outline lets you skip around more easily because you can see the whole plan easily.

* * *

And that's how to present your evidence—and how to cross examine your opponent's.

But what if you have something outside of the usual questions and answers to submit? Then, you need evidentiary predicates.

SHORT PREDICATES FOR SOME
COMMON KINDS OF EVIDENCE

How Do You Get Your Evidence Admitted? I've seen lawyers, particularly new lawyers, struggle over the predicate for business records, for example. They had Evidence courses in law school, but their classes hadn't included what lawyers actually have to do, unfortunately.

It Shouldn't Require Dozens of Questions. These predicates should be sufficient unless the judge is objection minded. I've almost always had these work. On two occasions, however, I've had judges sustain objections that my questions in evidentiary predicates were "leading," which they were, of course. This ruling is wrong. Rule 1101(d)(1) says that the Rules of Evidence don't apply to evidentiary predicates.

What if the judge sustains the objection and requires you to do it without leading questions? It may not be productive to argue with the judge and show Rule 1101. You'll just have to do it, and maybe he or she's got the right anyway to tell you the kind of proof he or she requires. It will take an enormous amount of time because most people don't stumble onto the pertinent answers without guidance. Try to tag your opponent with the wasted time. "All right, Mr. Witness, Mr. Opponent insists that we go by the book with this. It will take a lot of time, but let's do it."

What About Preserving Error? Be careful. In some cases, these predicates may not preserve error. They should, but courts are fickle.

Use Questions That Include the Words in the Rules. Imagine a lawyer who wants to establish the predicate for Exhibit No. 45, which is a business record. I suggest asking (see below), "Are records, including Exhibit 45, 'made and kept in the ordinary course of business' at your company?"[33] The phrase, "made and kept in the ordinary course of business" is derived from the Rule.[34]

Sometimes I think new lawyers are resistant to quoting the language that is inside the Rule. They've been taught not to copy, because copying is plagiarism. They instinctively want to be original. But the words of the rule are intended to be publicly used. It's not plagiarism to use them.

Translate the Question into Ordinary Language. After each question in the language of the Rule, state it in more common English. ". . . And by that I mean, Is this the kind of record your company usually makes and keeps?" Or something like that.

EXAMPLES OF WAYS TO OFFER EVIDENCE

A. A Business Record

"Now, Mr. Witness, I've got to ask you some technical questions. These questions are necessary because they fit the court's rules." *This is signposting.*

1. "Do you have care, custody, and control of records and documents like Plaintiff's Exhibit 67? And by that, I'm asking, are you the one who takes care of them?" (Yes.) *That second question amounts to translating it for the witness.*
2. "Are these records, including Plaintiff's Exhibit 67, made and kept in the ordinary course of business?" (Yes.)
3. "Was Exhibit 67 made originally and transmitted by a person with knowledge of the event recorded? And by that, I'm just asking whether a teller would have originally looked at the check when it was deposited." (Yes.)
4. "Was Exhibit 67 made originally at or about the time of the event recorded? What I mean is, did the teller record the deposit at the time it was in his possession? (Yes.)

B. A Prior Inconsistent Statement

The problem here is that sometimes jurors don't realize that the contradiction is the point. The first time I did this, jurors came up to me afterward and said,

---

[33] *See infra*, this page, the business record predicate.
[34] *See* Fed. R. Evid. 803(6).

"That was so confusing. It almost seemed like there were two different testimonies." I had to resist the urge to yell, "That's the point, you dummies! The witness was a liar!"

And so, I amended how I did it.

Step 1: Nail down the present testimony, given today. "So, you now claim that the light was red?" (Yes.) [The question asks, "Now," because this way it implies that he's told other stories; It asks about what he "Claims," because we know he's going to lie, but—heck, let's hear it.]

Step 2: Limit escape. "You saw it, didn't you? No way you could be mistaken?"

Step 3: Before asking the key question, build up the importance of telling the truth in the earlier statement.

"Do you recall coming to my office and giving your deposition? You don't go to a lawyer's office every day, do you? And so, it was a memorable occasion?" (Yes.)

"And the court reporter told you to raise your hand and tell the truth? And she took your words down on a little machine just like this lady's doing?" (Yes.)

"And if ever in your life you had to tell the truth, this was it?" (Yes.)

Step 4: Use the word "contradict" or "inconsistent" or both in asking whether today's testimony differed.

"But you contradicted what you said in your deposition, and you told it completely inconsistently today, didn't you?" (What do you mean?)

Step 5: Read the key answer yourself. "And on page 27, line 15, my question was, 'What color was the light?' and on line 16, you answered, 'It was green,' and so you contradicted your testimony today."

Step 6: Stop and go on to something else. Do not ask the witness to explain the contradiction. Do not ask, "Which one was it?" because that invites the witness to explain.

Step 7: Don't conclude that you've destroyed this witness. Jurors are forgiving of one incident like this.

C. An Expert Witness

I am assuming, here, that you have had a pretrial *Daubert* hearing (or whatever the expert witness law is in your state) in which the opinions of your witness have been ruled admissible.[35] Now you need to present the opinions to the jury, and that is what I'm concerned with here.[36]

You'll want to go over the witness's qualifications again, for the jury.[37] (I've had lawyers ask, "Do I give qualifications again, since I've already given them in the *Daubert* hearing?" The answer is Yes, of course, because the jury hasn't heard them yet, and the jury needs to know!) But jurors are usually interested, and you should develop the qualifications thoroughly.

Step 1: Qualifications. "What is your education? Your experience? Publications? Companies or government entities you've been a consultant to? Your certifications or licenses? Offices held? Recognition by way of awards or otherwise?"

I even liked to ask, "Have you mentored others?" (I'd suggest adding, "or taught other people who were newer?" because there will be jurors who don't know what "mentored" means.) People appreciate other people who are teachers. This little point makes the witness even more of an expert, and it shows him or her as altruistic.

Then, you go directly to the opinion.[38]

Step 2: Give the opinion first, as the rules allow. But don't use the word "opinion," because that word makes it sound uncertain. The jurors presumably can absorb the key message if it's presented first and in short form. So:

---

[35] Daubert v. Merrell Dow Pharmaceuticals, Inc, 509 U.S. 579 (1993).

[36] *See* General Electric Co. v. Joiner, 522 U.S. 136, 149 (1997) (concurring opinion of Justice Breyer) (suggesting "increased use of Rule 16's pretrial conference authority" to determine *Daubert* issues). He was right, and so, *Daubert* hearings have proliferated.

[37] Fed. R. Evid. 702-703 govern the qualifications of the witness, and they can depend on a broad array of characteristics of the witness related to the issue requiring expertise.

[38] Fed. R. Evid. 705 allows the expert to testify to the opinion "and give reasons therefor without first testifying to the underlying facts or data."

"Doctor, do you know, from your expertise, whether the carborundum in the coreopsis failed here? (Yes, I do know.)
The jury and the witness now realize that the big message is coming.

"And what is the answer to that?" (The carborundum failed, and that is what caused this accident.)

Step 3: Here, give the explanation for the opinion.

Why do it in this order? Some jurors will not follow the explanation, but they've heard the conclusion. Some other jurors may follow the explanation carefully, and they'll get it better if they've heard the conclusion first.

"Doctor, please explain to the jury how you arrived at this conclusion. What materials or documents about this case did you consider?" (Often, the answer will be, "I read all the depositions in this case.")

"And what was the first step in your reasoning?" "The next step?" (This pattern is workable for some kinds of experts. For others, it may be best simply to ask, "How did you arrive at your conclusion?")

Step 4: Give the original opinion again, summarizing what's gone before.

Step 5: Consider the arguments that the other side may make and show why it's wrong.

"Now, doctor, I'd like to discuss the claims Mr. Opponent is going to make. He wants to defend Bad Company by saying, contrary to your testimony, that the oxyquintonet cable to the coreopsis failed, and that is what caused the accident.

"So, please tell the jury why Mr. Opponent's theory is wrong.

Step 6: Give the conclusion again (third time).

"Now doctor, what is the correct conclusion? What was it that failed and caused this accident?"

If we discussed caveats, there would be many. For example, it is each of the individual opinions offered by the witness that are subject to the *Daubert* standard, not just the question whether the witness is some sort of expert.[39] Some opinions may be beyond what this witness can legitimately testify about, even if he's an expert.

Therefore, your opponent may object, and you may have skirmishes about many of the opinions, including perhaps the key opinion. You have to fight about these objections, but don't forget, the skirmishes interrupt and therefore muddle the testimony. You must also take care that the jury understands. Signposting again may help.

D. A Photograph or Drawing

"Now, Officer, I'm showing you what has been marked as Plaintiff's Exhibit 25.
"Can you tell us briefly what Exhibit 25 is a photograph (or diagram) of?"
(It's my drawing that shows the scene of the accident when I got there.)
"And does Plaintiff's Exhibit 25 truly and accurately show the scene as you saw it when you arrived? (Yes.)

:

The Rules allow many ways of authenticating exhibits,[40] and they are open ended, allowing other methods.[41] The words "truly and accurately" are not required. I suggest them because the judge has heard them many times and recognizes them. And you do not have to show a chain of custody, except in particular situations.[42] But if the judge requires it, you may have to show a chain of custody, and in some instances, it impresses a jury.

Ultimately, the standard is not demanding.[43] In fact, all it requires is evidence sufficient to support a finding, which is one of the lowest standards in the law.

A cautionary note: It's improper to show the exhibit to the jury before it's

---

[39] *Daubert* refers to the witness's "opinion" or "opinions" as the subject of its inquiry. *See Daubert,* 509 U.S. at 579 *et seq.*

[40] *See* Fed R. Evid. 901 (containing examples of what is sufficient).

[41] *See* Fed R. Evid. 901(a) (allowing any method sufficient to show that the item "is what its proponent claims."

[42] Dispensation with the chain has existed for a long time. *See, e.g.,* Alexander Dawson, Inc. v. NLRB, 586 F.2d 1300 (9th Cir. 1978).

[43] It requires only evidence sufficient to support a finding of authenticity. This is a low barrier, like the standard for a judgment as a matter of law or directed verdict. The judge does not need to be persuaded by a preponderance of evidence that the item is authentic. A prima facie showing is enough.

admitted. I know of no formal rule that says so, but it's a clear unwritten rule. It's common sense, and more importantly, if you don't follow it, the judge may admonish you in front of the jury with a voice of thunder.

E. An Object: The Murder Weapon, a Whiskey Bottle, Etc.

"Mr. Witness, I am showing you what has been marked as Plaintiff's Exhibit 103. What is it?" (It's a whiskey bottle that I retrieved from the defendant's car at the accident scene.)

"And how do you recognize it? By what details?" (I recognize the label, which is slightly discolored, and the fluid level, which is the same as what I saw before storing it in the police property room. I also see my initials on the label. I put those there at the time.") *Obviously, you don't need all these methods of authentication.)*

Then: "Your honor, I offer Plaintiff's Exhibit 103 as evidence."

And be sure to ask for a ruling that it is admitted if the judge doesn't immediately give one. Your record may not include it if you don't.[44]

---

[44] *Cf.* Guetersloh v. C.I.T. Corp., 451 S.W.2d 759 (Tex. App. 1970). There, the plaintiff's lawyer in a suit on a note omitted obtaining a ruling from the judge that the note was admitted. That presumably meant that there would have been no evidence to support the required elements of the claim. The appellate court saved the day. for the plaintiff by concluding that since all parties had treated the note as if it were in evidence, there was a kind of implied ruling admitting it.

Chapter 5

MOTION FOR DIRECTED VERDICT OR JUDGMENT AS A MATTER OF LAW

THE LAW GOVERNING THIS KIND OF MOTION

It's Called 'Judgment as a Matter of Law' in Federal Court. But it's still called a 'Directed Verdict' in some state courts. It's just terminology. The standard for both is really the same. The motion can be granted if the evidence allows only one possible judgment as a matter of law.

A Motion on the Issue During Trial, in Federal Court, is a requirement for a post-judgment Motion for Judgment as a Matter of Law. And for the issue to be raised on appeal, you must have made both motions. In some state courts, the rule is more relaxed.

It's a Happy Occasion if You Can Successfully make this kind of motion.

But the Judge May Withhold Granting the Motion during trial, even if circumstances allow it, and wait until the jury has decided the case. This is the careful approach. There are several reasons. The case need not be re-tried upon reversal because the court has the verdict; there is time for briefing after trial; the judge can grant the same motion after trial; and the jury may decide the case the right way and remove the need for the motion.

WHAT DOES THE MOTION LOOK LIKE?

In Some Courts, the Motion May be Made Orally. Be sure that the motion and the court's ruling are on the record. Then, the motion might sound like this:

> By Mr. Opposition: The Defendant, John S. Anton, hereby moves the court to grant a Directed Verdict providing that Plaintiffs take nothing for their suit and awarding costs to Defendant, on the following two grounds: that Plaintiff has failed to submit evidence, first, supporting any verdict that Defendant was negligent on the occasion in question or second, supporting any verdict that Defendant's conduct was a proximate cause of the occurrence in question.

To Which the Court Is Likely Simply to Reply: That's overruled.

If There Is Time to Put It Together in Writing, the Motion might look like this:

IN THE DISTRICT COURT
6TH DISTRICT OF WEST YORK STATE
NEW LONDON DIVISION

Meredith and Daniel Smith,
Plaintiffs

v.   No. _____

John S. Anton,
Defendant

DEFENDANT ANTON'S MOTION FOR DIRECTED VERDICT

Defendant John S. Anton hereby moves the court to grant a Directed Verdict providing that Plaintiffs take nothing for their suit and awarding costs to Defendant, on the following two grounds:

1. First, that Plaintiffs have failed to submit any evidence supporting any verdict that Defendant was negligent on the occasion in question; and

2. Second, that Plaintiffs have failed to submit any evidence supporting any verdict that Defendant's conduct was a proximate cause of the occurrence in question.

For these reasons, Defendant moves the court to grant this requested Directed Verdict.   [Signature and certificate of service omitted.]

Chapter 6

THE CHARGE CONFERENCE

WHAT HAPPENS AT THE CHARGE CONFERENCE?

Usually, at the End of All the Evidence, the judge will meet with the attorneys in chambers to hammer out the charge to the jury.

Will the Charge Be in Writing? The courts with which I'm familiar—both state and federal—give the jury written charges and verdict sheets, and they also read it all to the jury. I have heard of courts that just give oral charges. I can't imagine that—with the charge going out into the air, never to be seen by the jury. This chapter will assume that the charge is written.

Written Requests. If you want a particular charge included, write it as Request No.1 to Charge, and give the entirety of what you want at the charge conference. You can include Request No. 2, too, etc. The wording, of course, depends on your jurisdiction. See below.

Pattern Jury Carges Promulgated by the State, the State Supreme Court, or the Bar. These are documents displayed in books created by these organizations. They usually have been carefully researched to comply with the jurisdiction's law and, if they fit, are likely to be persuasive to the court. Familiarize yourself with these kinds of charges. In my state, there are several books containing different kinds of charges for each type of case, authored by the State Bar Association.

Submit a Complete Charge if You Can. Often you can submit a complete charge to the court. You do it so that the judge can adopt it as a whole, meaning that you've covered the standard definitions and verdict forms for the opponent, too. But there always are nuances here and there that aren't prescribed completely, and you word those so that the jury is likely to answer them in your favor. Better have authorities if you submit anything that needs them.

On the Record. Get your requests and the judge's ruling onto the record. This will make the issue more likely to be considered in connection with post-trial motions or on appeal. (Even if you don't expect to lose since you're using this book.)

Objections to the Charge. Immediately after the charge conference comes the time to object to the charge. The judge, of course, can't be expected to like this, but make sure you do it and do it on the record. This includes any charges of yours that the judge refused.

Try Not to Sandbag the Court by Objecting to Something You Didn't Raise at the Charge Conference. Imagine the scenario if you're the judge and you've squeezed together everything that fits from the charge conference, but now some jerk says you've got to go back and redo it. That's what it will look like to the judge. It happens sometimes in ways you can't prevent, but try not to do it.

AN EXAMPLE OF A COURT'S CHARGE
IN AN IMAGINARY JURISDICTION

This Charge Shows the Format and Method of a Charge. It shows standard instructions, definitions, and questions useful in a jurisdiction with comparative negligence. Note that it compresses all liability issues into one single question.

Do Not Use for Drafting. This charge should not be used for drafting. It is geared to an imaginary jurisdiction. Some jurisdictions may have similarly worded definitions and questions, or differently worded ones (for example, the definitions of negligence in California and Texas are differently worded although their meanings are substantially the same).

CHARGE OF THE COURT

MEMBERS OF THE JURY: This case is submitted to you on specific questions about the facts, which you must decide from the evidence you have heard in this trial. You are the sole judges of the credibility of the witnesses and the weight to be given their testimony, but in matters of law, you must be governed by the instructions in this charge. In discharging your responsibility on this jury, you will observe all the instructions which have previously been given you. I shall now give you additional instructions which you should carefully and strictly follow during your deliberations.

1. Do not let bias, prejudice or sympathy play any part in your deliberations.

2. In arriving at your answers, consider only the evidence introduced here under oath and such exhibits, if any, as have been introduced for your consideration under the rulings of the Court, that is, what you have seen and heard in this courtroom, together with the law as given you by the Court. In your deliberations, you will not consider or discuss anything that is not represented by the evidence in this case.

3. Since every answer that is required by the charge is important, no juror should state or consider that any required answer is not important.

4. You must not decide who you think should win, and then try to answer the questions accordingly. Simply answer the questions, and do not discuss or concern yourselves with the effect of your answers.

5. You will not decide an issue by lot or by drawing straws, or by any other method of chance. Do not return a quotient verdict. A quotient verdict means that the jurors agree to abide by the result to be reached by adding together each juror's figure and dividing by the number of jurors to get an average. Do not do any trading on your answers; that is, one juror should not agree to answer a certain question one way if others will agree to answer another question another way.

6. You may render your verdict upon the vote of ten or more members of the jury. The same ten or more of you must agree upon all of the answers made and to the entire verdict. You will not, therefore, enter into any agreement to be bound by a majority or any other vote of less than ten jurors. If the verdict

and all of the answers therein are reached by unanimous agreement, the presiding juror shall sign the verdict for the entire jury. If any juror disagrees as to any answer made by the verdict, those jurors who agree to all findings shall each sign the verdict.

These instructions are given to you because your conduct is subject to review the same as that of the witnesses, parties, attorneys, and the judge. If it should be found that you have disregarded any of these instructions, it will be jury misconduct and it may require another trial by another jury, then all of our time will have been wasted.

The presiding juror or any other juror who observes a violation of the court's instructions shall immediately warn the one who is violating the same and caution the juror not to do so again.

It is your duty as jurors to follow the law as I shall state it to you, and to apply that law to the facts as you find them from the evidence in the case. You are not to single out one instruction alone as stating the law, but must consider the instructions as a whole. Neither are you to be concerned with the wisdom of any rule of law stated by me.

DEFINITIONS

By the term "preponderance of the evidence" is meant the greater weight and degree of the credible evidence before you.

"Negligence" means a failure to do that which a person of ordinary prudence, in the exercise of ordinary care, would do under the same or similar circumstances, or the doing of something which a person of ordinary prudence, in the exercise of ordinary care, would not do under the same or similar circumstances.

By the term "ordinary care" is meant that degree of care which would be exercised by a person of ordinary care and prudence under the same or similar circumstance.

"Negligence," when used with respect to the conduct of a child, means failure to do that which an ordinary prudent child of the same age, experience, intelligence, and capacity would have done under the same or similar circumstances, or doing that which a similar child would not have done under the same or similar circumstances.

"Ordinary care," when used with respect to the conduct of a child, means that degree of care which would have been used by a child of the same age, experience, intelligence, and capacity under the same or similar circumstances.

By the term "proximate cause" is meant a cause which in natural and continuous sequence produces an event and without which the event would not have happened; and to be a proximate cause of an event it should have been reasonably foreseen and anticipated by a person of ordinary care that the event or some similar event would occur as a natural and probable consequence. There may be more than one proximate cause of an event.[**]

THE QUESTIONS

Question No. 1.
Did the negligence, if any, of the parties named below, proximately cause the death of Sarah Smith? Answer yes or no for each of the following:

(A)	Sarah Smith	Answer: _____
(B)	Meredith Smith	Answer: _____
(C)	John S. Anton	Answer: _____

If, in answer to Question No. 1, you found that the negligence of more than one of those named below proximately caused the death of Sarah Smith, then answer Question No. 2. Otherwise, do not answer Question No. 2.

Question No. 2.
What percentage of the negligence that caused the occurrence do you find to be attributable to each of those found by you in your answer to Question No. 1, to have been negligent?

The percentages you find must total 100%. Negligence attributable to a party named below is not necessarily measured by the number of acts or omissions found.

(A)	Sarah Smith	Answer: _____
(B)	Meredith Smith	Answer: _____
(C)	John S. Anton	Answer: _____

Total: 100%

[**] These definitions do not include unavoidable accident or sudden emergency instructions, which defendant should request in substantially correct form to preserve error. See Example Request at end of chapter, below.

If, in answer to Question No. 1, you have found that the negligence of John S. Anton proximately caused the occurrence, then answer Question No. 3. Otherwise do not answer Question No. 3.

Question No. 3.
Was such negligence of John S. Anton "gross negligence"? "Gross negligence" means such an entire want of care as to indicate that the act or omission in question was the result of conscious indifference to rights, welfare, or safety of the persons affected by it.
Answer yes or no.
Answer: _____

Question No. 4.
What sum of money, if any, if paid now in cash, do you find from a preponderance of the evidence would fairly and reasonably compensate Meredith Smith for her injuries, if any, which you find from a preponderance of the evidence resulted from her having seen the occurrence in question?
You may consider the following elements of damage, if any, and none other:
    (A)   Mental anguish suffered in the past.
    (B)   Mental anguish which, in reasonable probability, she will suffer in the future.
    (C)   Medical and therapy expenses in the past.
    (D)   Medical and therapy expenses which, in reasonable probability, she will suffer in the future.
    (E)   Loss of earnings and pecuniary value of her services in the past.
    (F)   Loss of earnings and service capacity which in reasonable probability, she will suffer in the future.
Answer in dollars and cents, if any. Answer: _____

Question No. 5.
What sum of money, if any, if paid now in cash, do you find from a preponderance of the evidence would fairly and reasonably compensate Meredith Smith and Daniel Smith for their loss, if any, resulting from the death of Sarah Smith?
Consider the following elements and none other:
    (A)   The lost earning capacity of the decedent;
    (B)   The loss of an inheritance, including what the decedent would have reasonably been expected to earn and gift had he or she lived;
    (C)   The loss of companionship, society, comfort, and love;
    (D)   The emotional pain and mental anguish suffered by survivors; and
    (E)   The lost value of household services.

Answer in dollars and cents, if any. Answer: _____

Question No. 6.
What sum of money, if any, do you find from a preponderance of the evidence would have fairly and reasonably compensated Sarah Smith for her conscious physical pain, if any, and mental anguish, if any, suffered before her death, as a result of the occurrence in question?
Answer in dollars and cents, if any. Answer: _____

Question No. 7.
Find from a preponderance of the evidence the reasonable amount of expenses for funeral and burial of Sarah Smith reasonably suitable to her station in life.
Answer in dollars and cents, if any.
Answer: _____

If, in answer to Question No. 3, you made a finding of gross negligence against John S. Anton, then answer Question No. 8. Otherwise, do not answer Question No. 8.

Question No. 8.
What sum of money, if any, should be assessed against John S. Anton as exemplary damages?
"Exemplary damages" means an amount that you may in your discretion award as an example to others and as a penalty or by way of punishment in addition to any amount that you may have found as actual damages.
Answer in dollars and cents for damages, if any.
Answer: _____

After you retire to the jury room, you will select your own presiding juror. The first thing the presiding juror will do is to have this complete charge read aloud and then you will deliberate upon your answers to the questions asked.

JUDGE PRESIDING

REQUESTING CHARGES: AN EXAMPLE

Separate Requests, Showing Sources. In my jurisdiction, it is wise to submit a whole charge but to request charges outside of that for instructions and questions that are uncertain.

The Law Applicable to Certain Defendant's Requests. In my jurisdiction, the defendant may be entitled to helpful instructions that are not included in the charge above. These instructions may include:

- Unavoidable Accident. Sometimes events are not caused by the negligence of any party; they are unavoidable accidents.
- Sole Proximate Cause. If plaintiff's conduct was the sole proximate cause, defendant's conduct could not have been a proximate cause.
- Sudden Emergency. If defendant was confronted with a sudden emergency that he did not cause, his conduct is judged as having occurred in the sudden emergency (such as a child darting in front of him).

A Sample Request for an Unavoidable Accident Instruction. Such a request might look like this:

Defendant's Request No. 1 for Jury Instruction or Question

Source: PJC 5.05.

Yarborough v. Berner, 467 S.W.2d 188 (State 1972) holds that when unavoidable accident is raised by evidence, the jury should be given an instruction on it. The PJC (Pattern Jury Charge) recommends this instruction. Defendant here requests that this instruction be given in this case to the jury:

An occurrence may be an unavoidable accident, that is, an event not proximately caused by the negligence of any party to it.

This request is granted / refused.

_____
District Judge

Chapter 7

JURY ARGUMENT

WHAT LAW AND CUSTOM GOVERN JURY ARGUMENTS?

Plaintiff Usually Has Two Arguments: opening argument and rebuttal. The defendant usually has one argument, sandwiched in between. Plaintiff's second argument is rebuttal, and theoretically it sounds as though it's limited to what the defendant has argued, but that nuance usually is not enforced. The legal theory is that this set of arguments compensates the plaintiff for having the burden of proof (and in rare cases where only the defendant has the burden, some state laws may reverse the order in favor of defendant).

A Powerful Advantage for Plaintiff. The plaintiff thus has the first and last word, which gives a big advantage to the plaintiff. The plaintiff gets to reply to everything, but the defendant does not. The plaintiff also gets to give the last speech before the jury retires.

Plaintiff's Usual Strategy in Opening. Given this order of events, the plaintiff's usual strategy is to give a straightforward and unemotional opening argument. The defendant's best arguments might otherwise come from excesses in the plaintiff's opening speech.

In the opening argument, plaintiff might cover the court's charge and give guidance on the answers to questions. The plaintiff can, for example, do a four-part treatment of each question: read it aloud, translate it into simple English, marshal evidence to show the desired answer, and tell how to answer it.

But plaintiff should not give emotional argument now. You'll get another chance, after the defendant finishes. That's when you give the emotional basis for the verdict you want. For now, just give a short, unemotional closing.

Defendant's Argument. Defendant's argument begins in a way that mirrors the plaintiff's argument. The defense attorney might begin by *very briefly* answering a couple of the plaintiff's arguments. (No more than two points, chosen not for their importance, but so that the offending argument and a definitive response can be given in two sentences.)

Then the defense might cover the court's charge and give guidance on the answers to the questions, but with the defense's spin. The defendant can, just as the plaintiff did, do a four-part treatment of each question: read it aloud, translate it into simple English, marshal evidence to show the desired answer, and tell how to answer it.

Lastly, the defense gives the emotional basis for the court's answers.

Plaintiff's Closing. Now, the plaintiff *very briefly* answers just a couple of defendant's arguments, chosen so that they can each be definitively stated and answered in two sentences. The plaintiff hits hardest on the biggest issues in the case. And finally, the plaintiff gives the emotional basis for the plaintiff's desired answers.

Emotional argument is necessary, according to that minor expert—me, the author. You can't evaluate negligence without it. You can't decide what is reasonable in balancing the safety of a child against the freedom to ride a motorcycle without it. Aristotle said that persuasion needs *logos, pathos, and ethos.* Logic, emotion, and authority. The emotion has to be there, so get ready to shed that bloodless law school analysis and whip up some emotion.

OUTLINING A SET OF FINAL ARGUMENTS

If we were to make an outline of a set of final jury arguments, it might look like the following:

I. Plaintiff's Opening Argument
A. Thank you, jurors: you've been attentive, and we know you've concentrated.
    You're part of the American system of justice.

B. I will go over the court's charge. Not my words—the court's.

C. Preponderance of Evidence, court says—[read definition]. [Stand with arms outstretched; scales of justice.] Means greater weight.

    Just a little wiggle upward [demonstrate with arms] is preponderance.

D. Negligence, court says—[read definition]. See, it's a departure from ordinary care. Negligence is carelessness.

E. Negligence of children, court says—[read definition]. Children aren't adults. We hold them to lesser standard.

G. Proximate cause, court says—[read definition]. Honestly, in a case like this, prox. cause just means, "What really caused this tragedy?"

    And that's the court's definitions. Very simple. Straightforward, this is a simple case.

H. Now, the court asks you questions . . . Also, very simple.

    [With each question:
        > Read it;
        > Translate it into regular English;
        > Marshal the evidence in your favor; and
        > Tell the jury the proper answer.]

    1. First Question asks you [read it] "Did the negligence, if any, of the parties named below, proximately cause the death of Sarah Smith? Answer yes or no for each of the following." And there are answer blanks for little Sarah, Meredith, and John Anton.

    [Translate into English] Now, that just means, "Who was careless and caused this tragedy, taking into account that little Sarah was six years old?"

    [Marshal the evidence toward Anton only] John Anton was driving at 50 to 65 mph at 3:15 in a school zone. We have 2 overlapping witnesses. He is the only one whose negligence caused this tragedy. Little Sarah was only six. Why do we have school zones? Because we know that children don't know as much as adults. Meredith was in her fenced backyard. Sarah wasn't negligent. She didn't cause her own death. Meredith wasn't negligent.

    [Tell answer] The only one who answers this question is John Anton.

I. Read, translate, marshal evidence, and tell answers for all the other questions too.

J. And that, Ladies and Gentlemen, is really all that this case is about.

II. Defendant's Argument

A. I also want to thank you, jurors . . .

B. I don't see the case the same way as Mr. Garrison.

C. [Pick out two vulnerable arguments made by plaintiffs. State each in one sentence and answer it in one sentence. You don't want to have the other side's argument guide your own argument.]

D. The judge's instruction on negligence isn't what Mr. Garrison said at all. [Read the definition.] You see, the word "carelessness" isn't in there at all. What it says is that to be negligent, you have to be *guilty* of an *unreasonable act*.

E. Mr. Garrison left off an important instruction, namely that an event can be an unavoidable accident. [Read the instruction:] "An occurrence may be an unavoidable accident, that is, an event not proximately caused by the negligence of any party to it." John wasn't negligent.

F. And I also don't see the questions the same way as Mr. Garrison.

[Here, the defense lawyer goes through the questions and

1. Reads each one;
2. Translates it into simple English;
3. Marshals the evidence so that Meredith and Sarah are negligent, but not John; and
4. Tells the right answer.]

So, Question 1 asks [read it]: "Did the negligence, if any, of the parties named below, proximately cause the death of Sarah Smith?" And there are answer blanks for Sarah Smith, Meredith Smith, and John S. Anton.

[Translate into simple English:] What that means—Who was guilty of an unreasonable act and proximately caused this accident?

[Marshal the evidence in favor of John] Mr. Garrison conveniently leaves out the testimony of Ms. Elaine Nardone—followed right behind John. The testimony of John himself. They both said that John was going slowly, less than 20 mph. The testimony of an uninvolved party—Ms. Nardone—who was right there—is more believable than testimony from Meredith Smith, who's emotionally involved, and Officer Hauseshorn, who didn't see the event. Meredith didn't walk her daughter home or teach her child how to cross the street. Sarah darted out into the street.]

[Tell the right answer:]

Sarah and Meredith were negligent but not John.

G. [Give the emotional basis for defendant's position] This lawsuit is just wrong because it's wrong for someone who's not negligent to be called that horrible name, "negligent," in a lawsuit. John was going slowly, but it only takes a bunch of paper for anyone on earth to accuse him and try to saddle him with damages that will ruin his life.

The amount they're claiming, they can turn this little girl's death into money to buy municipal bonds, tax-free, and live high on the hog for the rest of their lives. This lawsuit is just trying to find a scapegoat and get revenge against somebody. It's wrong to chase after revenge like that.

III. Plaintiff's Closing Argument

A. [Hit hardest on the major issues:]

Mr. Opponent is dead wrong. John Anton was going way, way, beyond the speed limit. The witnesses to that fact are clear, and they overlap. The body of this poor child, little Sarah, made three blood spots over 105 feet, longer than a third of a football field, like a stone skipping across water.

And for him to ridicule the proof of damages is also just plain wrong. What do you think the value of a human life is worth? EPA has studied it and uses $ 10.5 million. It should be more for a child who has many more years to live than an average adult. But our request is careful: just 10 million.

B. [Give the emotional basis for plaintiffs' position:]

Why do we have school zones? To protect our children, who are our future. We can't have lawbreakers like John Anton deliberately violate the speed limit there. The results of his ignoring the law are seen in these grieving parents. They have lost countless numbers of wonderful things in the growth of their baby child, like putting ornaments on the Christmas tree together. And the future: school, college, and some day walking her down the aisle. The loss is unimaginable and enormous.

LAWYERS' STRATEGIES AND TACTICS IN JURY ARGUMENT

This advice is taken from an article that I wrote several years ago, but it still holds up today.[45]

I. Plaintiff's Opening Argument.

[Plaintiff's first argument] is not an occasion for histrionics [because the defendant's argument will follow, and plaintiff will have a final opportunity in rebuttal] . . . Your opponent's best points may come from points you exaggerate.

[An outline of a well-organized argument, if special interrogatories are used, might look something like this:]

A. *Introduction.* This [part] consists, often, of thanking the jurors and setting the stage. "It has been a long trial . . . I want to thank you for your careful attention during it. I am a fan of the jury system, because I think it does more substantial justice than any other system devised on earth . . . You are here today to say who is responsible for the accident. . . ."

B. *Explanation and Emphasis of Legal Considerations* [*In the Charge*]. "I want to go over the judge's charge with you. And . . . I want to remind you of the [voir

---

[45] David Crump, *Effective Jury Argument: The Organization*, 43 Tex. B.J. 468 (1980).

dire] examination, in which I told you that the court would define certain terms for you. Here's the court's definition of the term 'negligence,' for instance (read the definition) . . . [I]t comes down to this: If a person . . . is careless—that is negligence. And what this defendant did certainly fits the definition. . . ." In the same manner, cover each of the other legal issues you want to emphasize. Simplify them in a manner favorable to the conclusion you are trying to guide the jury toward. . . .

C. *Take the Special Interrogatories, One by One, and Go through Four Steps.*

(1) Read the Question, (2) Translate It into Simple English, (3) Marshal the Evidence Toward the Conclusion You Want, and (4) Tell the Jury the Finding You Believe It Should Make.

> (1) The first special [interrogatory] asks this: "Do you find from the preponderance of the evidence that the defendant [was negligent]?"
>
> (2) All that means, ladies and gentlemen, is, was the defendant careless. . . ?
>
> (3) . . . And what does the evidence show? First of all, he plowed right into the plaintiff's car . . . Second, the damage to the car is severe. That indicates undiminished speed. Third, the witnesses say he swerved only at the last minute. Fourth, the defendant's own testimony—with a little prodding from me—tells you that he saw the plaintiff when he was just about ten feet away.
>
> (4) [Very humbly] I would suggest to you that the answer should be Yes. . . .
>
> Now, special [interrogatory] number two asks you. . . .

Ordinarily, it is not good [strategy] to . . . summarize the evidence by going through what the first witness said, what the second said, and so forth. The evidence should be marshaled in a way that answers the questions the jury will have to answer.

D. *Make a Short, Unemotional Closing.* "I ask you . . . for a verdict that answers the questions the way I have just described . . . I believe it is supported by the evidence. . . ."

You have the right to close. Don't shoot off your biggest emotional guns now.

II. Defendant's Argument.
Defendant has the disadvantage of having his entire argument sandwiched between the plaintiff's two arguments. Therefore, he must combine all of his points in one

argument.

A. *Introduction.* This phase of the argument . . . might be very much like the plaintiff's introduction. . . .

B. *Answer . . . the Opposing Argument—In Short Fashion.* You have to answer the plaintiff's argument. However, you should not let the plaintiff's argument dominate yours . . . Answer and get it over with. . . .

1. Tell the jury you are going to answer . . . [But:]
2. Tell the jury . . . you are not going to try to answer everything. "I'm not going to have time to answer every single point in the plaintiff's argument, because he has raised such a number of them. It's a scattershot argument."
3. Explain your adversary's role. "Mr. Jones, the plaintiff's lawyer, is of course representing the plaintiff. I have no quarrel with that . . . But I think you have to realize that everything he said was calculated to get a recovery for the plaintiff . . ."
4. Answer one or two points—briefly. "He tells you that the plaintiff is a young man, in the flower of his youth. That is an attempt to make you feel sympathy. ... But what has the judge told you? 'Do not let bias, prejudice or sympathy play any part in your deliberations.' . . . He also tells you that the witnesses said John swerved at the last minute. Well, the answer to that, and Mr. Jones conveniently leaves it out, is that the child darted out in front of him suddenly. . . ."

C. *Having Answered Briefly, Say:* "Now, I Want to Get Down to What This Lawsuit is Really About."

D. *Go Over the [Instructions] and the Special [Interrogatories]. But Not the Way the Plaintiff Did; the Way You Think They Should Be Answered.* "The judge tells you that negligence means 'unreasonable' conduct. Now, I just don't think [the evidence shows] John was guilty of any unreasonable conduct." . . . Then go over the special [interrogatories] individually, marshaling the evidence and giving the answers you believe appropriate [which will be the opposite ones from the plaintiff].

E. *Give the Jury the Emotional Basis for Holding for You.* "Ladies and gentlemen, anybody can sue anybody else. There's not even a screening panel that decides whether the lawsuit has any merit to it . . . The only protection John here has is you, even if he's completely right himself. It will be a terrible thing if, every time somebody pulls out in front of you suddenly and your car hits them because of it, you get sued for damages. . . ."

F. *Tell the Jury That Your Opponent Has the Last Word—You Can't Answer.* "In a moment I'll sit down, and I won't be able to answer Mr. Jones . . . He may get emotional . . . If he does just remember this: Emotionalism is the indication of a weak argument. He may distort things . . . I must trust you, and I do; and if he says something wrong, you will recognize it."

III, Plaintiff's Closing Argument

Plaintiff may begin with an answer to the defense argument. It should take a form similar to the defendant's answer to the plaintiff, above. Then the plaintiff's lawyer should:

A. *Go Over the Issues Again, More Briefly This Time, Again Marshaling the Important Evidence.*

B. *Hit Hardest on the Fundamental Issue in the Case.*

3. *Give the Jury the Emotional Basis for Holding in the Plaintiff's Favor.* "When you're injured by someone else's carelessness, the law is very simple. If they refuse to assist you in bearing the cost of your injuries, you come before a jury of your peers and ask for justice. No person is an island. We are all responsible for assisting those whom we have injured . . . carelessly by our inattention, as the defendant did. His efforts to pin the blame on the plaintiff are disgraceful . . . The plaintiff will go through the rest of his days with a part of his life taken from him. This is his only day in court for that [loss]. I pray you—I beg you: Do not turn a deaf ear on his plea for simple justice."

* * *

And with that, you've tried your jury trial. Now, you can enjoy the dubious pleasure of sweating the jury.

APPENDIX

A MODEL FOR YOUR TRIAL NOTEBOOK

Here Is a Case that We Use Throughout the Book. Plaintiffs Daniel and Meredith Smith are suing John Anton. The plaintiffs' witnesses say that Anton drove his motorcycle in a school zone at 3:15 p.m. at speeds estimated at 50 to 65 mph by a police officer, Officer Hauseshorn, and by Meredith Smith. He collided with little Sarah Smith, their six-year-old daughter, and killed her while she was walking home from school. They have an economist and themselves to testify to damages, which they claim exceed $10 million.

Anton's defense includes a witness who followed Anton, who will testify that Anton was going slowly, under the 20-mph speed limit. The child darted into the street, he claims, and he couldn't stop. The defense also says that the damages claim is way exaggerated.

So, Here Are Excerpts from the Notebook.

[Part 1, first page: Witness Contacts]

WITNESSES

1. Meredith Smith 555-118-1234, 555-888-0123, 2700 Maple Lane 77027

---

2. Daniel Smith 555-118-1234, 555-888-0122, 2700 Maple Lane 77027
3. Professor James Q. Noddingly (Economist) 555-281-2234, 555-173-2201, 555-173-0118, 2399 Campus Blvd 77002, 1818 University Offices # C-143
4. . . .
5. . . .

[Part 1 cont., Motions]

1. Motion in Limine
2. Renewal of Motion for Severance
3. . . .

IN THE DISTRICT COURT
6TH DISTRICT OF WEST YORK STATE
NEW LONDON DIVISION

Meredith and Daniel Smith,
Plaintiffs

v.   No. _____

John S. Anton,
Defendant

PLAINTIFF SMITHS' MOTION IN LIMINE

Plaintiffs Daniel and Meredith Smith request the order in limine set out below, and would show:

1. There are facts about settlement and insurance that would be extremely prejudicial if mentioned or implied before the jury.

2. Therefore, plaintiffs request that the court enter the order attached to this motion as Exhibit A.

[Signature and delivery to other party omitted.]

EXHIBIT A

IN THE DISTRICT COURT
6TH DISTRICT OF WEST YORK STATE
NEW LONDON DIVISION

Meredith and Daniel Smith,
Plaintiffs

v.   No. _____

John S. Anton,
Defendant

ORDER IN LIMINE

It is ordered that neither party shall suggest or imply to the jury any information about

1. the existence of any kind of insurance protecting any party from any kind of expense or obligation, or any materials or speech relating thereto, or

2. The existence of any settlement negotiations, settlement offers, or materials relating to settlement or negotiations between these parties or any others,

Until and unless any party has obtained a hearing outside the presence of the jury admitting and allowing any such suggestion or implication.

_____
West York District Judge

[Part 2, Notes for Voir Dire]

1. Thank the potential jurors
2. Defendant drove his motorcycle 50-65 mph . . .
   A. Negligence is
   B. It just means *carelessness*

. . .

[Part 3, Opening Statement Outline]

Good morning, Ladies and Gentlemen . . . .

I'd like to thank you, jurors . . . .

[See Chapter 3 for an outline and advice on the Opening Statement.]

[Part 4, Witness Examination Outline]

MEREDITH SMITH

1. Name
2. Orientation Q: You are a plaintiff, and you're here to tell about the horrible accident that killed little Sarah; is that right? [See Chapter 4.]
3. Her background. [See Chapter 4.]
4. . . . . See Chapter 4 for advice on Witness Examination.

[Part 5. Motion for Directed Verdict (or JMOL)]

[See Chapter 5 for an example. Put this document here if there is any prospect for it.]

[Part 6. Jury Instructions and Verdict Forms]

[See Chapter 6 for an example. Insert this document here.]

[Part 7. Notes for Final Arguments to the Jury]

[See Chapter 7. Insert this document here.]

qp

Visit us at *www.quidprobooks.com*.